Social Work Macro Practice Workbook

Exercises and Activities for Policy, Community, and Organization Interventions

---

David P. Fauri

F. Ellen Netting

Mary Katherine O'Connor

VIRGINIA COMMONWEALTH UNIVERSITY
SCHOOL OF SOCIAL WORK

Australia • Canada • Mexico • Singapore • Spain
United Kingdom • United States

Executive Editor: Lisa Gebo
Assistant Editor: Alma Dea Michelena
Editorial Assistant: Sheila Walsh
Technology Project Manager: Barry Connolly
Marketing Manager: Caroline Concilla
Marketing Assistant: Mary Ho
Advertising Project Manager: Tami Strang
Project Manager, Editorial Production: Candace Chen
Art Director: Vernon Boes
Print Buyer: Barbara Britton
Permissions Editor: Stephanie Lee
Production Service: Virginia Somma
Copy Editor: Simone Payment
Cover Designer: Denise Davidson
Cover/Text Printer: West Group
Compositor: Stratford Publishing Services, Inc.

Printed in the United States of America
1 2 3 4 5 6 7 08 07 06 05 04

Library of Congress Control Number: 2004102000

ISBN 0-534-51303-4

Thomson Brooks/Cole
10 Davis Drive
Belmont, CA 94002
USA

Asia
Thomson Learning
5 Shenton Way #01-01
UIC Building
Singapore 068808

Australia/New Zealand
Thomson Learning
102 Dodds Street
Southbank, Victoria 3006
Australia

Canada
Nelson
1120 Birchmount Road
Toronto, Ontario M1K 5G4
Canada

Europe/Middle East/Africa
Thomson Learning
High Holborn House
50/51 Bedford Row
London WC1R 4LR
United Kingdom

Latin America
Thomson Learning
Seneca, 53
Colonia Polanco
11560 Mexico D.F.
Mexico

Spain/Portugal
Paraninfo
Calle Magallanes, 25
28015 Madrid, Spain

Contents

Preface

We have viewed the process of assembling and writing this workbook as both an opportunity to influence the future development of new social workers and an opportunity to review and revise materials and processes we have developed and used in our own teaching over a period of many years. We have also challenged ourselves to create new materials that emphasize present-day social work education and social work practice goals.

Authenticity is a concern for us. Most of the exercises and activities found in this workbook are classroom tested and as closely related to real-life situations as possible; many are based on real incidents or events. We believe that instructional materials based on real situations and experiences add immensely to the classroom experience and learning of social work students who want real-world learning experiences and can hardly wait to encounter practice. Experiential learning helps to meet this desire while also helping with the transition from classroom to practice. We sought to ensure that each exercise or activity fits the realities of social work practice and the needs of those teaching and studying it. As students have pointed out to us, *doing* social work is more fun than reading about it, and exercises and activities can be akin to actually doing social work!

Our intent is to provide teaching–learning materials that recognize both the instructional needs of, and challenges facing teachers, and the learning needs and demands of motivated students. We especially wish to reinforce social work education's emphasis on critical thinking, cultural competence, and ethical sensitivity. Designed to recognize the complexity of macro practice, the book contains exercises requiring students to develop their critical-thinking skills, build cultural competency, and identify and define ethical issues. The materials found here allow for problem-solving experience in a protected environment. Students can thus try out decision making and fast-paced or time-restricted responses to policy, community, and organization situations, while having a second chance for learning through the debriefing and corrective feedback that are not often available in actual practice. Analytical and decision-making skills are used in most every exercise and activity included here. The target audiences for the exercises and activities are M.S.W. foundation students and upper-division (junior and senior) B.S.W. students. Some instructors may also find the materials appropriate for introductory work with Advanced Macro Practice M.S.W. students in the areas of policy practice, community practice, and organization practice.

Materials from policy, community, and organization arenas of practice offer a broad sampling of the almost unlimited number of issues that can arise in social work practice. Connections between macro and micro practice can be illustrated with many of the exercises and activities. The vignette ("The Days of Our Placements") that continues throughout section introductions is intended primarily to introduce specific practice arenas and methods. It is an unfolding story that can be used as a discussion vehicle in the classroom. The last chapter contains material useful in helping students to identify for themselves their future professional roles and leadership potential.

We expect that you may feel the need to skip around in the workbook or use some parts and not others. In fact, we suspect the freedom to choose between exercises will be a major strength of the workbook. We hope both instructors and students will take advantage of the tear-out page format and three-hole-punched pages to facilitate review and feedback availability for future reference. We believe there is much joy—for both instructors and students—in teaching and we hope instructors and students have a rewarding experience using this workbook.

Acknowledgments

We thank many colleagues who supported our efforts. We acknowledge and appreciate the interest and encouragement of Lisa Gebo, Social Work Editor for Thomson Brooks/Cole. To Frank R. Baskind, Dean of the Virginia Commonwealth University School of Social Work, we acknowledge resource support, even in tough budget times. We also would like to thank the following reviewers for their comments and suggestions: Jeff Schrenzel, Western New England College; Katherine Shank, graduate student at Northwestern University; Vicki Gardine Williams, Tennessee State University; Susan W. Gray, Ellen Whiteside McDonnell School of Social Work, Barry University; Carol L. Langer, University of Nebraska; Maria Roberts DeGennaro, San Diego State University; Dennis Cogswell, Radford University; Richard Edwards, University of North Carolina, Chapel Hill; Jean Kruzich, University of Washington.

We extend significant thanks to our students with whom we have used earlier versions of most of these materials. Their engagement and serious participation helped to convince us of the efficacy of this project and provided critical feedback that strengthened the materials you are about to read. We also wish to thank Sheila Walsh of Thomson Brooks/Cole and Virginia Somma of Stratford Publishing Services.

About the Authors

We favor teaching with experience-based instruction methods in B.S.W. and M.S.W. courses. We also favor working collaboratively and prefer to introduce ourselves in terms of what we have produced together and enjoyed working on together, but conventional format and clear communication goals dictate individual summaries.

David P. Fauri is Professor of Social Work at Virginia Commonwealth University (VCU) where he teaches courses in the M.S.W. foundation curriculum and advanced M.S.W. concentration in administration and planning, doctoral social-policy seminars, and introductory B.S.W. courses. He has been at VCU for 20 years, having taught in and administered social work programs previously at the University of Tennessee, the University of Kentucky, and Southern Illinois University at Carbondale. He has served on the Board of the Council on Social Work Education, been active in leadership in the National Association of Social Workers in Virginia and Tennessee, and has served on numerous local community, city, county, and state-level boards, including Parents Anonymous, United Way, and public social services. He is active in local government politics. Previously, he planned and developed community programs for elders in state and local government and consulted and trained in public and United Way bodies, as well as serving in the Peace Corps in Nigeria. Publications include a number of journal articles and book chapters, as well as various training and evaluation studies. His most recent work includes *Cases in Macro Social Work Practice* (2000; revised 2003), with Stephen P. Wernet and F. Ellen Netting. He serves on the editorial board of *Arête,* is a consulting editor for the *Journal of Social Work Education*, and is a regular reviewer of book proposals and journal manuscripts.

F. Ellen Netting is Professor of Social Work at Virginia Commonwealth University where she teaches in the M.S.W. program in the area of macro practice, policy, administration, and planning, and in the B.S.W. program in which she teaches a course on oppressed groups. She has been at VCU for 10 years, having previously taught for 10 years at Arizona State University. She continues to collaborate with Dr. Peter M. Kettner and Dr. Steven L. McMurtry on *Social Work Macro Practice,* now in its third edition (2004) with Allyn & Bacon. She is the coauthor of six additional books and has published more than 100 book chapters and refereed journal articles. She received the VCU Distinguished Scholar Award in 1997 and was elected to the National Academy of Social Work Practice as a Distinguished Scholar in 1998. Her scholarship has focused on health and human service delivery issues for frail elders, as well as nonprofit management concerns, primarily in religiously affiliated agencies. Recently she completed a project funded by The John A. Hartford Foundation as part of a national demonstration on primary care physician practice in geriatrics, in conjunction with an interdisciplinary team of researchers. She serves on the editorial boards of *Nonprofit Management and Leadership, The Journal of Applied Gerontology, The Journal of Gerontological Social Work,* and *The Journal of Religious Gerontology* and reviews articles for numerous journals in the areas of social work, nonprofit management, and aging. Her latest book is *Organization Practice.*

Mary Katherine O'Connor is a Professor in the School of Social Work at Virginia Commonwealth University where she has taught in the M.S.W. and Ph.D. programs for 15 years. She received a B.S. in Art from Immaculate Heart College, Hollywood, CA, and M.S.W. and Ph.D. degrees from the University of Kansas. Prior to entering academics, Dr. O'Connor was a member of the Peace Corps in Brazil and has extensive direct and administrative practice experience in child welfare in government and the nonprofit sector. She was a Fulbright Scholar in Brazil where she taught constructivist research and conducted research with street children. She was the director of a child welfare stipend program that prepares B.S.W. and M.SW students for careers in public child welfare practice. Her present research involves assessing the impact of a sexual abuse prevention intervention and understanding effective models of faith-based service delivery in urban settings. She is a member of the National Association of Social Workers and the Council on Social Work Education where she is a member of the Women's Commission. She is the coauthor of *Evaluating Social Programs,* with Dr. Netting, coauthor of *Organization Practice,* and the sole author of *Social Work Constructivist Research*. She has written numerous journal articles with a particular focus on child welfare issues or constructivist research methods. She is a consulting editor for *Social Work* and on the editorial boards of the *Journal of Progressive Human Services* and the *Journal of Qualitative Social Work Research and Practice* and reviews articles for several other journals in the areas of family violence, child welfare, and qualitative methodology.

A Note to Students

As you proceed through this workbook you will encounter brief orientating introductions, similar to this one, at the beginning of each major section: Critical Thinking; Policy Practice; Community Practice; Organization Practice; and Leadership and Professional Development. Within each section you will also find a vignette featuring a set of students. If you wish to catch up with what has happened with the student workers in the vignette, return to the introductory part of the previous section and reread the developments presented there.

We designed the workbook to allow users to engage in small-group exercises and classroom discussions, as well as individual activities. Activities call for you to apply your creative and critical reading/thinking skills individually. Exercises call for group interaction and group problem-solving skills. Because there is often overlap in individual and group skills, you may not always be aware of which is being emphasized at a given moment. That is to be expected; what is important is that the exercises and activities add to or reinforce the repertoire of competencies for professional social work practice. We also should note that some exercises and activities primarily emphasize development of knowledge, skills, and value-oriented insights while others also may add an evaluative element. They call on you to demonstrate and summarize what you have learned and what you can do related to macro practice interventions, allowing you and your instructor to review and check your progress.

At the beginning of each part of the book, we provide a summary chart. Charts are organized according to increasing levels of expertise: (1) demystification, (2) conceptualizing and defining, (3) increasing sensitivity, (4) practicing related tasks, and (5) enhancing change skills. Demystification introduces the area of practice that will be covered in the section and is followed by activities or exercises that develop your conceptual and defining abilities. Increasing sensitivity targets a higher level of consciousness through completion of exercises and activities that are considered related to practice. Last, enhancing change skills includes more complex exercises and activities. The summary charts also point out the separation between exercises (intended for group or classroom use), and activities (targeted to individual learning).

We enjoyed developing these exercises and activities, and we want you to have fun using them and learning from them. Many were created and then refined in classroom and small-group situations over a number of years. Others were created especially for this workbook. Learning materials such as those found here should never remain static—that is, they should change constantly, just as practice and the environment of practice constantly change. We welcome your reactions and suggestions concerning what you like and what you do not like in the workbook, and we are especially interested in knowing what helps to make you a better social work practitioner.

And now, let's begin.

"The Days of Our Placements: Scene I"

At the beginning of the semester in their Integrating Field Instruction Seminar (or IFIS as it was known among the students), Tamara, Harry, Chrystal, Yusof, and Maria sat around the table looking at one another. It was time for the first seminar session to begin, but no instructor was present. They did not know one another, although they had seen each other in the halls from time to time.

Tentatively and almost to herself Chrystal mused, "What do you do if the instructor doesn't show?"

Tamara replied, "Well, at some schools they do what is called 'bolt,' but only if the class has not started after fifteen minutes."

A bit uncertain, Chrystal responded, "It is only seven minutes after the hour, let's give it the additional eight minutes."

There was a nervous pause before Yusof chimed in, "We really can't do that to a professor. There is probably a good reason."

Harry had been studying the situation carefully, taking his time before speaking. Sensing everyone's uncertainty, he suggested that they use the time to advantage and get to know one another.

Masking her nervousness with words, Tamara quickly rattled off, "Well, I'm Tamara and I'm in my second year of study, coming here from a small farming town in Georgia. I wanted to go into child-welfare work and now have to since I have a child-welfare stipend that requires me to work in that field for two years for each year of sponsorship."

Maria, who had not yet said a word, seemed to realize that she had better get with the program. She shyly added, "I really wanted one of those, but I lost out. I'm happy just to be in school as I'm the first one in my family of seven children to have that privilege." She smiled at the others as she added, "Oh, my name is Maria . . . "

As Maria told them her name, Harry blurted out, "you sound like you must be from the city, like me."

Taken aback, Maria replied, "Yes, I'm from Bogotá; but I haven't lived there since I was a little girl."

"Oh, sorry," Harry inserted quickly but not particularly apologetically, "I'm from New York City and lots of people there seem to sound like you, but most of them are more or less connected to Puerto Rico."

At this point, Maria glared at Harry, as Yusof came into the discussion, saying "What about me? Do you wonder where I'm from? I happen to be from Yemen, but you probably can't tell that. My name is Yusof."

Chrystal, looking a bit lost by this time, said in a bright way, "Well, I'm from right here—high school, college, the whole bit, and this is the best place you could ever want to be, isn't it?"

Harry, who looked to be older than the others, replied, "Aren't you a bit, er, young to conclude that?" Now Harry had a second female glaring at him!

To the relief of all, in walked their professor, apologizing for being late and saying she hoped they had the opportunity to make good use of the time. On hearing that they had "sort of gotten to know each other," she indicated she would then use the remaining time not for introductions, but to discuss the field-placement agency to which they were being assigned. She said she could get to know them during individual conferences at the agency. She started the discussion with what seemed to the students to be a sort of warning: "We want to consider the importance of thinking critically and not jump to any conclusions about this agency, which you will be getting to know quite well, or about the people it serves and the problems they face. In fact, this is not unlike thinking carefully and critically about relationships in our personal lives and the need for cultural sensitivity with those with whom we live and work." As she paused, silence fell in the room.

Part 1
Critical Thinking

Keywords:
contextual decision making
critical reading
critical thinking
critical writing
cultural competence
cultural destructiveness
decision making
ethical absolutism
ethical decision making
ethical dilemmas
ethical relativism
leadership
multiple perspectives

Introduction

We begin this workbook with what many people would consider to be a generalist practice perspective because we believe that competent large-systems intervention is possible for, and required of, all persons educated as social workers, no matter the type of practice in which they engage.

Given our belief, we first focus on good contextual decision making. Contextual decision making is defined as a process of being aware of all the forces (e.g., social, political, economic) that surround what one decides to do in any professional social work intervention and the careful consideration of the consequences of the actions one decides to take. Note that contextual decision making about policy, organization, and community issues is necessary whether one is working with an individual or a group of people. We identify three building blocks essential to contextual decision making: (1) critical thinking, (2) cultural competence, and (3) ethical decision making.

At the end of this workbook, you will also be exposed to another very important element of professional practice—leadership. Together, contextual decision making and leadership make possible effective professional policy, community, and organization practice.

This introductory section provides exercises and activities that will aid you in managing the complexity of social work macro practice. Starting with critical thinking as a first building block for everything that follows, you will move from simple to complex thinking on a variety of issues. Opportunities for critical reading, critical thinking, and critical writing are offered to engage you in dealing with multiple perspectives and their consequences. Throughout this process, the power of language will become clear as terms that comprise the language of social work macro practice are introduced.

Recognizing the power of language is central to fully appreciating the second building block—cultural competence. We will push beyond understanding societal oppression and its consequences and help you make practical efforts to understand your own viewpoint, working from your current viewpoint to a place of acceptance and respect for difference. Each of us begins this process at a different place, depending on our own unique life experience. Various frameworks will be offered to help you develop personal awareness of your beliefs about differences. Also included are ways to assess large systems, including organizations, communities, and human-service delivery systems, so that true cultural competence can be addressed in planning and carrying out interventions. We also want to reduce the potential of engaging in, due to lack of insight and knowledge, cultural destructiveness and incapability as parts of social work macro practice. We hope that through engaging in the exercise and activity opportunities provided in this workbook your own competence will increase.

The third building block is ethical decision making. We place the ethics portion of this introductory section last because we believe that critical thinking and cultural competence are essential to ethical practice and often come into play in situations requiring judgment about ethical matters. In addition, we recognize that personal and contextual values are relevant for professional ethical behavior. Using the workbook, we hope you will develop the ability to understand when ethical dilemmas exist and then, using critical thinking and cultural competency, be able to move from a personal stance to a professional social work stance.

"The Days of Our Placements: Scene II"

As a hush fell over the room, each student contemplated their first placement experience. The professor continued with her introduction to the agency.

"This agency is a former settlement house, and it has a long and at times distinguished history. It just had a centennial celebration, although it has not been a settlement all 100 years. In fact, the past 50 years have seen it function as a community center, and it is now known as Community House. Other things have also changed. A major difference is that while at its founding its client base was mostly immigrants, Catholic and Jewish, from central and eastern Europe, today the client population is mostly Latin and African American."

On hearing this, Harry, never reticent, added a comment, "Such agencies were really important 100 years ago. My family still tells stories that concern the Jewish Settlement House in New York City that my grandparents frequented when they came to America."

The professor nodded an acknowledgment and continued. "In the 1940s, times changed and as the community around the agency began to change from one with a European tradition to one of African-American heritage, the agency sought United Way funding for its programs and tried to find a new identity for itself. These were not easy times, but it continued to serve those who were establishing themselves in what to them was a new land—people like Harry's grandparents. The profession of social work was also changing, and Community House engaged in grassroots community organizing. For a period in the 1960s, the staff spent a good deal of energy challenging 'the establishment.'"

Critical Thinking: Exercise and Activity Chart		
Focus	**Exercises**	**Activities**
Demystifying Critical Thinking		Activity A: Reading Skills Activity B: Ethnic Identity Activity C: Diversity
Conceptualizing and Defining Critical Thinking	Exercise 1: Defining Social Justice	
Increasing Critical Thinking	Exercise 2: Socioeconomic Class and Oppression Exercise 3: Social Distance Exercise 4: Historical Perspectives	Activity D: Self-Awareness and Race Activity E: A Continuum of Awareness
Practicing Critical Thinking	Exercise 5: Theories Exercise 6: The Workplace Exercise 7: Ethics	Activity F: Complex Thinking
Enhancing Critical-Thinking Skills	Exercise 8: Constructive Confrontation Exercise 9: Assessing Presentations Exercise 10: Beginning Problem Statements Exercise 11: The Whistle-Blower Exercise 12: The Chief Financial Officer Retires Exercise 13: Unique, Intelligent, Condemned	Activity G: Planning for Personal and Professional Safety

Critical-Thinking Exercises

Critical-Thinking Exercise 1

Defining Social Justice

In a small group of three or four students, define social justice. Compare the definitions of each of the small groups and then create a definition that captures the thoughts of the full class.

Return to the original small groups and using the class definition of social justice do the following:

1. List five major social injustices in American society.

____

____

____

____

____

2. Select one of the social injustices, record your decision-making process that establishes this as your primary agenda, and develop change-strategy options for overcoming that injustice.

____

____

____

____

3. Select another one of the social injustices and identify the barriers to change you would anticipate encountering.

____

____

____

____

____

Meet in the full class again to compare findings.

Critical-Thinking Exercise 2

Socioeconomic Class and Oppression*

This group exercise is based on the concept of social stratification and the six major class strata in the United States, using one way in which socioeconomic class could be categorized. Divide the class in the same way the general population is:

1. Upper Class = .5 to 1%
2. Corporate Class = .5%
3. Upper-Middle Class = 10.5%
4. Lower-Middle Class = 31.5%
5. Working Class = 42%
6. The Poor = 15.1%

Accomplish the division by creating an appropriate number of slips for each class category based on the total number of students in the class. For example, in a class of 29 students, the breakdown would be: 1 upper class; 1 corporate class; 3 upper-middle class; 9 lower-middle class; 11 working class; 4 poor. Each student selects a slip and finds others in their class in order to form a group. The upper- and corporate-class representatives may talk together or remain alone for the exercise.

Each group should respond to the following questions:

1. How does it feel to be assigned to this particular class?

____

____

____

____

____

____

____

2. As a member of this class, what do you think your chances are of obtaining equal access to the list of social–economic goods below?

 - Societal rights/liberties and equal protection under the law

____

____

 - Income and wealth

____

____

*(Special appreciation to Dr. Michael Sheridan, Associate Professor, Virginia Commonwealth University, for her work on this exercise.)

- Education

- Housing

- Community and family safety

- Health care, including mental health and substance-abuse services

- Adequate nutrition

- Leisure pursuits and secure retirement

- Nature, culture, and beauty

- Experiences that enhance self-respect and personal empowerment

3. As a member of this class, what do you think your chances are of obtaining protection from the following list of societal problems?

   - Community and family violence

   - Substandard housing/homelessness

- Malnutrition and hunger

- Pollution and hazardous wastes

- Hazardous working conditions

- Crime

- Arrest and incarceration

- Acute diseases, chronic medical conditions, physical disabilities

- Premature death

- Prejudice and discrimination

4. What do you think your chances are concerning social mobility, both upward and downward, given your designated class status? What other factors might play a role in your chances for social mobility?

Come back together to share the small group discussions as a class. Be sure to focus on both the informational and affective dimensions of the experience in order to get the best exposure to much of the real-life feelings and experiences of the various social classes.

Critical-Thinking Exercise 3

Social Distance

In 1926, Emory S. Bogardus[1] developed the Bogardus Social Distance Scale to assess the extent to which people are willing to enter into close relationships with those different from themselves. In the following exercise, respond to the ethnic groups as they are mentioned by assigning a number from the following scale adapted from the work of Bogardus.

1 = Would marry
2 = Would have as a regular friend
3 = Would work beside in an office
4 = Would have several families in my neighborhood
5 = Would have merely as speaking acquaintances
6 = Would have live outside my neighborhood
7 = Would have live outside my country

The ethnic groups under consideration are:

- White
- Irish
- Jewish
- African American
- American Indian
- Japanese
- Mexican American
- Arab
- Chinese
- Cuban
- Vietnamese
- Haitian

(Other ethnic groups currently in the news can be added.)

1. Obtain a mean, mode, and range for each ethnic group.
2. Rank the groups in the order of distance, closest to furthest on the scale.
3. Analyze the results for intended and unintended consequences.
4. What are the social-justice implications of your results?

---

[1]Bogardus, E. S. (1959). *Social Distance.* [s.n.] Los Angeles, CA. Reprinted, Yellow Springs, OH: The Antioch Press.

Critical-Thinking Exercise 4

Historical Perspectives

Review the five-column table that follows. It puts macro social work practice into an historical context with organization theory. In small groups, first consider why the items mentioned happened within each time frame. For each item in the "Questions" section, draft a short answer or response. Be prepared to share your responses with the entire class.

Historical Perspectives on Planning and Administration, and Organizational Theory

Time Period	What Was Happening in the Profession of Social Work	What Was Happening in the Development of Organizational Theory	Things to Consider	Questions
Early 1900s	Profession emerged in Progressive Era. First schools were forming. Charity Organization Societies (COS) & Settlement Houses were in place. COS workers prided themselves on being "scientific."	Rationality prevailed as U.S. became more industrialized and urbanized. The workplace had shifted to the organizational arena. What are now called "classical theories" prevailed.	Foci on social casework (called retail social work) and social reform (called wholesale social work) were reflected in COS & Settlement House movements.	How was rationality defined?
1915	In 1915, National Conference of Charities & Corrections featured Abraham Flexner.	Flexner represented traditional authority as defined by Weber.	Flexner lumped social work with the "semi-professionals" such as nursing, teaching, and library science.	Why did the profession embrace Flexner's authority?
1920s	First textbook on community organization (CO) appeared. Debate between grassroots advocates and persons focusing on policy development and agency-based provision of services increased. Radical social work movement emerged.	Mary Follet and social work educators such as Eduard Lindeman called attention to the role of primary groups in local communities. Hawthorne Studies were conducted. Proliferation of private human-service agencies occurred.	Rationality prevailed, but there were quests for community and studies that led to Human Relations theory. Human Relations theory recognized the "informal" system at work within organizations.	Why would there be increasing tension between grassroots advocates and agency-based providers? Why did a radical social work movement emerge? Why were there so many voluntary agencies?
1930s–1940s	Radical social workers participated in the Labor Movement. The profession embraced Freud. Social workers also entered public service jobs as the "welfare state" emerged.	Welfare provision became dominated by public organizations.	Critics of rationalistic, mechanistic approaches to organization moved toward human-relations approaches.	Why the shift from voluntary to public provision of services? Why the preoccupation with Freud?

1960s	Many social movements came to fruition, providing opportunities for CO and community development (CD). Government programs expanded. In 1962 the Council on Social Work Education (CSWE) recognized CO as a method of social work practice comparable to group work and casework. Schools of social work rushed to establish CO curricula.	With growth in size and complexity of organizations, fiscal accountability became a growing concern in human service organizations. Late 60s marked the emergence of the organization in its environment, obsession with uncertainty, and open systems theory.	Growth in concern over fiscal accountability led social workers to assume administrative positions and become "managers." Implicit in this shift was the move from external focus on social problems and community to internal focus on budgetary and operational efficiency.	What are the implications of open-systems theory on organizational thinking? What does a focus on efficiency mean for the provision of social services?
1970s–1980s	Tracks in administration and planning were available in many schools of social work. Recognition that governmental services were highly bureaucratic and were limited led to increased purchase of service contracting and beginning reprivatization efforts.	Organizational culture and other alternative frameworks became obsession of popular management literature.	Social workers witnessed trends toward conservative approaches as Reagan's presidential term began.	Why did so many alternatives emerge, and how integrated into social work curricula are these approaches? How do social work planners and administrators maintain a social justice orientation in contemporary practice? Why is there a micro–macro split in the profession?
1990s–present	Reforms in social welfare and increasing efforts to dismantle established services were the focus of much professional attention. Faith-based initiatives emerged in the public arena. Calls for recognizing the connections between macro and micro social work replaced previous tendencies to dichotomize practice into macro and micro.	Organizational culture became a part of the accepted literature. Empirically based pieces that tested were organizational theories increasingly published. Acceptance of nonprofit studies proliferated as did nonprofit management programs.	Professional identity concerns were voiced as nonprofit programs increased. Social work students in various universities gained access to nonprofit programs often housed in public adminstration, business, or in social work programs.	Why would nonprofit programs be more and more common at this time? How has the identity of social work changed by the turn of the century? How have organizations dedicated to advocacy and social justice fared in the last decade?

Critical-Thinking Exercise 5

Theories

In a small group, choose a theory that has been discussed in class. As an aid in developing a strategy for studying and thinking about that or any other theory or theoretical framework, try to answer the following questions. If you do not have a clear understanding or definition of what a theory is, discuss that before choosing the theory.

1. What theory have you selected?

2. What are the basic concepts of the theory?

3. Who are the major proponents of the theory?

4. What is this theory's explanation of individual, family, group, or societal problems?

5. What is this theory's approach to individual, family, group, or societal strengths?

6. What suggested goals for change might be derived from the theoretical perspective?

7. Identify examples of change strategies that might be used for individual, family, group, or societal change that would be congruent with the assumptions of the theory.

8. What are the limits of the theory?

Critical-Thinking Exercise 6

The Workplace

Critical thinking in the workplace is an important element of organizational assessment, problem analysis, understanding communication and power, and planning for and implementing change. In a small group try to develop your own frameworks for thinking about and understanding the above. Consider what would be important questions to be answered in thinking about the workplace. Think about what information might guide your assessment and diagnosis for effective practice.

1. Organizational assessment: What should one look for regarding organizational structure and behavior?

2. Problem analysis: What should one be sure to include in an effort to understand an organizational problem with organizational structure or behavior?

3. Workplace communication and power: What important elements should guide one's efforts in understanding standards of communication and the use of power within the organization?

4. Planning for and implementing change: What information should be collected in order to determine if change is possible within the organization?

5. Once feasibility has been determined, what should be considered in order to assure implementation and institutionalization of the change?

____

____

____

____

Critical-Thinking Exercise 7

Ethics

Divide the class into teams and read the scenarios. Each team should select a particular scenario and then answer the questions listed below.

Scenario A: Working with Staff

The secretary in your agency is a struggling single mother who is intelligent and quite able. Lately she seems to drift a bit. She is not totally focused on her work; she seems quite jumpy and sometimes out of sorts. You are concerned about her as a person, but you are also tired of having to double-check her work. You have talked to her about the quality of work you expect from her, but not much seems to have happened. Because you are not considered her direct supervisor there is not much else you can do. You have now been asked to provide feedback on her performance by her supervisor. Should you give specific information regarding her lack of attention and competence? You know that you will be required to sign any document you provide regarding her work and any complaint might be shared with her directly. Could this further erode your working relationship? If others are having the same experience this evaluation could put the secretary on probation with the possibility of being fired.

Scenario B: Working with Colleagues

The last couple of times you have been with your colleague, a senior social worker, you think you have smelled alcohol on her breath. You have begun to notice that she always seems to be popping peppermint candies in her mouth. You also notice that she seems to be much more nervous or reactive in tense situations lately. Several times in the last couple of weeks her office door has been shut (which is a big change; she has been the most open and available of all staff members) and when you have knocked it has taken her a few seconds to open what appears to have been a locked door.

Scenario C: Working with Clients

As an ongoing social worker you make an unannounced visit to a family who has become known to the agency for child neglect. No formal charges have been filed because so far there has been insufficient evidence to determine the existence of neglect. However, during the investigation the family seemed chaotic and really willing to accept help to better serve the three children under 5. Today when you go to the house, it is dark, even though it is after 10:00 a.m. When the mother comes to the door she seems a bit disoriented and not totally awake. There is no indication that anyone else has gotten out of bed. In addition, you smell marijuana.

For each of the scenarios, consider the following questions:

1. What are the ethical issues (societal, personal, professional)?
2. What criteria should be used to resolve the ethical dilemma (efficiency, effectiveness, rights, others)?
3. Who should resolve the issue and why? What should be the solution?
4. Who benefits from this solution and where are the potential conflicts within the proposed solution (society, client, profession, others)?
5. What are the ethical consequences of options discussed? Can we assume the proposed resolution presents the least harm?
6. Are there other issues that should be considered, given your understanding of the ethics of the social work profession?

Critical-Thinking Exercise 8

Constructive Confrontation: Critique without Criticizing

Social work macro practice sometimes requires confronting issues or individuals in order to bring about desired, positive change. As an expressive skill, confrontation is a form of individual and group communication that calls attention to and/or challenges another person and/or existing conditions. Unfortunately, it is all too easy to compromise one's best intentions in this regard in order to bring about desired outcomes. The **DON'T** rules below represent some of the negative behaviors that can create barriers to achieving desired results, and the **DO** rules are intended to help achieve results.

In small groups, for each of the **DON'T** points below, identify an example of real-life professional situations in which **DON'TS** were employed. Identify the negative consequences of each. Be prepared to share this with the entire class.

For the **DO** list, select from the list of **COMMUNICATION FORMS** one approach for each of the six items and prepare samples of constructive confrontation phrasing to share with the entire class.

The DON'T List

Don't criticize anything that cannot be changed. There is no point in raising a concern that can only result in hardening of positions.

Don't criticize past mistakes. Water over the dam should be just that, over and done with, as it also can result in hardening of positions, thus inhibiting change potential.

Don't hurt the other person in subtle or obvious ways.

When you must say "No," don't feel or act guilty. That is part of the job.

The DO List

Do suggest options that give others choices in bringing about the desired change.

Do build from strength. Identify what is already right and build on these positives.

Do remember that people usually criticize themselves (perhaps too much).

Do remember that people recognize and are sensitive to their own mistakes and that they may be willing to correct them.

Do offer hope for the future.

List of COMMUNICATION FORMS

1. Light challenge (I wonder?)
2. Direct frontal attack (Cut the bull!)
3. Favorable and pleasant (Positive)
4. Unfavorable and repugnant (Negative)
5. Respecting individual's humanness (Unconditional)
6. Symbol of direct contact—verbally or nonverbally (Stroking)

Critical-Thinking Exercise 9

Assessing Presentations

For all social workers, macro practitioners in particular, it is important to have excellent public speaking/ persuasion skills.

This exercise is to be used during in-class presentations as an opportunity to apply skills in judgment that one would use in practice. Try to answer each question relating to a presentation made in class. This can provide a base for constructive feedback to presenters and be of help to you in planning for your future presentations.

1. Is the purpose of the presentation clear? Why or why not?

___

___

2. Is the presentation consistent with what the audience expects?

___

___

3. What language and metaphors are employed in the presentation?

___

___

4. Are the language and metaphors relevant to social work values?

___

___

5. Is the structure of the presentation audience-sensitive?

___

___

6. Are language, metaphors, and structure inclusive of and sensitive to diverse groups, without being so focused on process that outcomes are disregarded?

___

___

7. How does this presentation address the possibility that some groups or individuals will find elements of the presentation offensive?

___

___

8. Is the presentation grounded in practice reality? Whose reality is recognized?

___

___

9. What feedback would you give the presenter about the quality of the presentation?

____

____

10. What feedback would you give the presenter about the manner in which she or he presents?

____

____

Critical-Thinking Exercise 10

Beginning Problem Statements

This exercise contains six vignettes drawn from real practice situations. These examples all have a main point or statement to make. For each vignette below, evaluate the statement by asking these questions:

- Who is the target population?
- Is this a subgroup of a larger target population?
- What are the community boundaries?
- What are the organizational boundaries?
- Is this a problem or a condition statement?
- What would you change about this statement?

1. When incarcerated offenders are transferred between facilities in different jurisdictions or when they are released, they are not adequately prepared to make this transition. It is reported that 30% of these ex-offenders have communicable diseases and do not have access to the health resources they need. Therefore, resources are needed to plan for and transition ex-offenders back into the community.
2. Children with disabilities and their families in New Town are suffering due to lack of highly skilled and trained child-care providers. It is estimated that there is a 40–60% turnover rate in child-care staff. It is necessary to intervene so that providers can give the best care possible to children with disabilities and their families.
3. At-risk youth between the ages of 16–21 in New Town have limited and inadequate resources to support them in becoming independent adults. Some of these youth have no or few natural supports. There is a need to provide support for these youth as they transition into adulthood.
4. Disabled homeless families in Garden City who have serious mental illness, chronic alcohol and other drug problems, AIDS, or a combination of these disabilities need shelter in order to survive. Case managers report that clients do not know how to perform basic instrumental activities of daily living. Appropriate life skills must be learned in order to remain in the community.
5. Students in Carsonville affected by crisis events and not receiving immediate counseling and support are at risk for experiencing increased psychological trauma and adapting negatively to the crisis. Negative adaptations to crisis events may take the form of social isolation, depression, drop in school performance, substance abuse, or cluster suicide. There is a need for professionals to respond to crisis events affecting students in a timely and organized fashion.
6. Increasing numbers of older persons and their families in the United States are faced with decisions about long-term care, for which they are not adequately prepared. As the current population of frail elders (age 85 and above) increases and chronic conditions worsen, crises often force these decisions. Resources need to be devoted to preparing consumers for making informed decisions.

Critical-Thinking Exercise 11

The Whistle-Blower

Dr. Jones was incredibly likeable. She was admired by office staff. Nurses and social workers who worked with her were in awe of her abilities. Patients warmed to her compassionate bedside manner. She was moving up in the national arena, being seen as a person on the "conference circuit" who everyone wanted to appear as their keynote or plenary speaker.

Dr. Jones was addicted to prescription drugs. At first, no one suspected. She would fall asleep in team meetings and she was losing weight. Staff fretted over her, thinking that she was working too hard. Everyone was protective of her.

The news of Dr. Jones's addiction broke when a nurse blew the whistle on her. The nurse thought that the physician was overprescribing for some patients. When she got up the nerve to ask Dr. Jones about this, Dr. Jones told her not to worry. She tried to relax at these reassurances, but she was unsettled. After weeks of concern, she blew the whistle by taking her suspicions to a hospital administrator.

An investigation ensued. The hospital put Dr. Jones on leave. No one knew why, and most everyone assumed that she was very ill. Staff worried about her having been terribly overworked. Rumors spread that maybe she was dying, for she looked so unhealthy. Everyone felt sorry for Dr. Jones.

For months, charges were pending and no one knew what was happening. Staff who had loved Dr. Jones were either in disbelief or assumed she had been falsely accused. When the local newspaper reported that she had been indicted, some people were angry at her. The nurse who had turned her in felt "used" because she had been asked to get the drugs from the cabinet and give them to Dr. Jones. She had thought they were for patients, certainly not for Dr. Jones's use. The nurse shared her concerns, frustration, and anger with the social worker.

As a group, carefully examine the issues of power and ethics in this situation. Use the following questions to guide your process.

1. What kind of power does Dr. Jones have and why?
2. What kind of power does the nurse have and why?
3. Even after the facts are known, why are some people so conflicted over what has happened with Dr. Jones?
4. If you were the nurse, how would you feel about being a whistle-blower?
5. If you were the social worker, how would you help the nurse deal with her feelings?
6. What ethical issues arise in this case?
7. Are there other power issues in this case?

Critical-Thinking Exercise 12

The Chief Financial Officer Retires

Florence Withers felt she had served Safe Haven well for twenty years. She knew she was a creative person and that in addition to doing a good job as chief financial officer, she had provided leadership in the adoption of several innovative approaches in nonprofit agency management. She had found social-agency management to be more rewarding than the corporate finance work she had left when she was 40 in order to pursue an M.S.W. degree. In fact, she was very pleased with the career she had made for herself.

These are the matters Florence is considering as she arrives at the office on this special, final day on the job before she retires. She reflects on her recent accomplishments while glancing, as is her habit, at the local morning paper, *The Daily,* which is folded next to the cup of good coffee on her desk.

Suddenly she is dumbfounded and surprised to see a front-page article featuring Safe Haven. The article raises the specter of a sweetheart deal and implies that as she retires she is receiving a financial package that outstrips anything any local nonprofit agency has ever provided, one that would be hard to beat in the corporate community. According to the reporter, Mary Wallace, who authored the article and who usually covers local political news, the only similar situation that could be recalled involved a local university that "employed the same tactic for a retiring vice president." The article also mentions that donors giving to local social service agencies might be affected if the public were to associate such tactics with loose management practices such as occurred in the national United Way of America scandal a few years earlier.

Florence thinks to herself, "Wow, this is *quite* a way to go out," and she sits down with coffee in hand to ponder her last management innovation for the agency that, as it is turning out, may have brought about this unsettling newspaper article. She recognizes her rational thought process kicking in, as it had done many times in the past 20 years. She knows she needs to have the facts and the history well in hand before even beginning to think about how, or if, to respond. Her initial thought is that this was to have been a win–win situation that would benefit the agency's stakeholders—clients, community, staff, and to a small degree, her retirement plans. To herself, she mumbles, "Isn't that the way progress is made?"

Florence recalls that when she initially proposed creating the Safe Haven Foundation, it was understood by all involved that the purpose was to provide an independent source of revenue for Safe Haven. It was anticipated that the Foundation would, and should, take on special financial arrangements such as the one under question in the article. In fact, she had made the idea of "flexible investment" a big part of selling the concept. She had borrowed the idea from higher education when she observed public universities working around funding constraints and limitations imposed by state budgets and public laws by creating university foundations to pursue fund-raising through non-publicly controlled investments and purchases. Some even used their profits to supplement the salaries of the university president.

"Really," she thought, "it was a stroke of genius for the Foundation to buy my house from me as an investment." Of course, this was the first time the Foundation had purchased a personal residence, let alone the home of an agency staff member, with the intent of reselling it and making a profit. Even if it was Florence's house, that should not change the complexion or the intent of the Foundation to invest money for Safe Haven's benefit. After all, Florence was not an employee of the Foundation, and the Foundation had been intentionally set up to be independent of Safe Haven! Even if she wanted to be rid of the house now so she could move to a retirement community and reinvest the money in a home there, it was still a good, legitimate investment for the Safe Haven Foundation. All the Foundation had to do was to hold the property until a fair market price could be obtained in the fall, since selling now (in January) would not result in the best price. Potentially, a profit of $10,000 could accrue through the Foundation for agency purposes. She again went over her thoughts of several weeks ago. She had thought that she was making a final contribution to the agency and (humorously) that it was too bad she could not also claim a tax deduction for a charitable contribution since she was benefiting the agency. In a sense, she had offered the Foundation an opportunity to gain $10,000 to benefit Safe Haven.

Couldn't *The Daily* have had the courtesy to talk to the Foundation or Safe Haven? After all, it could easily be shown that this was a win–win situation and that it was perfectly legal. To top it off, the article did not mention that the Foundation had made money on every investment it had made to date, including some commercial property. At this point, Florence's emotions began to come to the fore as she thought, "because I was going to be able to move to the retirement community sooner rather than later there was no reason to go off half-cocked and imply that there was something shady going on!" In creating the Foundation, she had seen to it that the bylaws and investment decision procedures were reviewed and given careful scrutiny not only by the agency board and the State Corporation Commission but also by the legal department of a local corporation that had its own foundation. Further, she had recruited the Foundation board of directors from some of the most respected business, corporate, and financial institutions in the community.

The cup of good coffee was gone now, and Florence knew from experience that even though it was really very good coffee, there was a price to be paid later if she had another this early in the morning. She also asked herself, "What other prices might have to be paid today?" Well, at least this final day on the job was not going to be boring. With this passing through her mind, she picked up the phone, pulled her keyboard toward her and began . . .

Class Discussion Questions

1. Identify the characters involved in this scenario.
2. What is the setting? Where does the action take place?
3. What is the time frame of the action?
4. What is the essence of the story line as the case progresses?
5. Are situational ethics involved in this case?
6. Might Florence have identified a potential ethical issue as this situation was developing?
7. Do you think questions of personal ethics or professional ethics are involved in this situation?
8. What observations would you make concerning the meshing of Florence's personal life and her professional career?
9. Assume that what has been done is done, but that the future is still in front of us. How might you handle this situation if you were sitting in Florence's chair as she picks up the telephone and pulls the keyboard toward her? Develop an outline for the next paragraph of the story:

Now divide the class into three groups and have each group consider Florence's story from four different perspectives:

Group 1:

Imagine that you are Florence. After retiring from the agency, you are reviewing what took place as you drive to your new home after the sale of your previous home. This is the first time you have had enough distance, in both space and time, to be able to reflect on what took place. You try to answer these questions:

- Did you handle the sale of your house to the Foundation too much on the quiet?
- Was there someone from whom you might have gotten a second opinion before doing so?
- What might have been done to reduce possible perceptions of impropriety?

Group 2:

Imagine that you are the administrative team of Safe Haven and that you, with the help of the board and staff, have put things back together after the public and media blowup over your retiring CFO. You ask yourself what went wrong and how you as an organization can prevent this sort of thing from happening again in the future. You see this as an opportunity for organizational learning and conclude that you should explore policy options.

- What are some of these options?
- Over what time period(s) might these options be put in place?
- Are some options temporary in nature and some more permanent?
- What are some issues that might be involved in implementation?

Group 3:

Imagine that you and a group of M.S.W. students have observed what has happened through reading the newspaper accounts and discussing them in practice class with the guidance of a concerned professor. Being in the enviable position of being outside observers, how would you respond to the following questions raised by your professor?

- If you were pushed to describe a type of ethical choice that Florence faced, would you consider this to be a question of professional ethics or one of personal ethics?
- Were situational ethics involved?
- Is an ethical dilemma found here? That is, was Florence faced with a situation necessitating choice between apparently equally important values?
- Beneficence is a motivator for many persons in the social services. Is that a value that possibly comes into play in this case?
- Does the principle of autonomy come into play in any way in this case?

Group 4:

Imagine that you are Mary Wallace. Tell the other participants in this exercise:

- Why you wrote this article. (Remember that it may have been assigned to you by the editor since you usually cover local political matters.)
- Why didn't you contact the agency, Safe Haven, before writing the article?
- Why didn't you contact Florence?
- Would you welcome contact from the agency at this point, after the article's publication? Why might the agency want to contact you?

Critical-Thinking Exercise 13

Unique, Intelligent, Condemned

This exercise is intended to help you distinguish between ethical relativism and ethical absolutism in your professional assessment of situations. Ethical absolutists argue that basic principles do not change and that there are overriding universal values that will withstand the test of time. Ethical relativists say there is no one truth. Rather, principles and values change with time and context. This applies to all levels of systems practice (e.g., individuals, groups, organizations, communities).

Read the following article that could have appeared in your local daily newspaper and as a group, answer the questions that follow.

1. Are there any issues in this story that disturb you as a professional social worker? (Think in terms of the child welfare information, the drug use/treatment information, the criminal justice information, and the apparent role of a professional social worker.)
2. What are the ethical principles that apply?
3. Taking an ethical absolutist position, what are the ethical problems and the rules that apply?
4. Taking an ethical relativist position, do the same sort of analysis.
5. Determine the consequences of applying different ethical rules or ranking these rules differently.

UNIQUE, INTELLIGENT, CONDEMNED

Those who met Petulla Ann Missmer, who is currently on death row while appeals continue, saw that she was a crafty survivor. Those knowing her for some time understood that she had potential beyond what she had accomplished. "She is unique, intelligent, and condemned," said a local advocate for women in prison, Gueniver Bogge, a social worker now acting as a child-welfare lobbyist. Bogge knew Missmer when Missmer was a member of a substance abuse recovery group Bogge organized and led while directing a human-service agency.

Bogge commented that Missmer was well intentioned and wanted to be a good mother to her child, who had suffered possible brain damage that may have been related to Missmer's addiction while pregnant. Friends who bring the child to the state correctional facility for women for biweekly visits with Missmer confirm that she is interested in and concerned for the child. To some, and especially those advocating for a reversal of the death sentence facing her, this interest in and commitment to her child is paramount to her future.

Baby Anne, as she is called, is now three years old, having been born while her mother was in prison for the murder of the child's father in a fit of passion after finding him with another woman. Ms. Missmer has admitted to having had several problems, including drug use, shoplifting, and passing counterfeit bills. She, however, continued to deny involvement in the death of the child's father, who died under the wheels of a train, apparently having been pushed there while intoxicated. Friends say that it is a tragedy that Baby Anne faces life with limited mental capacity, as well as without her mother.

Before entering prison just over three years ago, Missmer was a capable treatment-group member and actually helped organize some of the group's activities, according to Bogge. However, Bogge also said that "she could con you and most anyone into believing that she was capable of anything asked of her, and in the group sessions the leader had to confront her with this image of competency that she created. I knew she was pregnant, and I tried to help her see that she could not deal with a child the way she was dealing with the rest of the world." Bogge added that Missmer was extremely depressed when she learned that she was going to be indicted for the death of the child's father and that she desperately sought a godparent for the child, which she never found. The child was placed in foster care where she remains. Bogge says that she was the one who called the child welfare department to begin foster care arrangements but now wishes she had arranged to take the child herself.

Missmer's court-appointed lawyer is preparing an appeal to the Governor. A time schedule for the appeal and the Governor's decision is not currently available.

Critical-Thinking Activities

Critical-Thinking Activity A

Reading Skills

The following are questions that will help you fully engage with the material from your reading assignments in a critical way. Choose an article or a reading assignment for any of your classes. Read it in whatever way you would usually read to prepare for class (straight through, reading for themes, underlining, writing in the margins, taking notes, and so on). When you have finished, answer the following questions:

1. What was the key theme(s) and major point(s) of the article or book section?

2. What did you learn that was new (new information/idea or new way of thinking about an issue)?

3. What did you know already that was reinforced or supported by the reading?

4. What questions did the reading raise/generate? (These might be points of disagreement, concepts that were not clear, or places where you saw the need for specific data to justify and support assertions.)

5. What feelings did the reading generate? What was the source within you for this response (values, beliefs, experiences, fears, frustrations)?

6. What did you see as connections/applications from this reading to content in other social work classes? To your social work practice?

Critical-Thinking Activity B

Ethnic Identity

Spend some time thinking about your personal and family background and then answer the following questions:

1. What is your ethnic background? To what ethnic group(s) do you belong?

2. In the community where you grew up, besides your own ethnic group, what other ethnic groups resided there?

3. Describe the advantages you and your family may have experienced due to your ethnicity.

4. Describe the disadvantages you and your family may have experienced due to your ethnicity.

5. What are your earliest memories of color as an ethnic factor? Is this memory positive or negative? How does it connect with your current relationship with color and ethnicity?

6. How would you evaluate your ethnic group in terms of power?

Analyze your responses to determine if there are themes that suggest that changes might be warranted. If there are themes, develop a plan of action for change.

Critical-Thinking Activity C

Diversity

This activity is designed to get you in touch with your own culture, and potential sources of internalized oppression and/or pride. Create a picture of your own life experiences that could be said to have created your self-identified culture.

1. What is your ethnicity (ancestral origin)?

2. What have been your experiences with racism or ethnocentrism?

3. What has been your experience with sexism or a sense of entitlement?

4. What is your socioeconomic class? What has been your experience with classism?

5. What is your age? Have you experienced ageism?

6. What is your first language? Do you speak any other languages? What has been your experience based on your language patterns, dialect, or accent?

7. What is your level of education? Is that level "normal" in your family/community?

8. What is your religion and/or spiritual belief? What has been your experience related to pressure for and against your religious or spiritual position?

9. Where were you born? Have you experienced any positive or negative stereotyping due to this?

10. What is the composition of your family? What is your relationship to your family? What negative and positive elements about who you are can be related to your family of origin?

11. What is your sexual orientation? What has been your experience with heterosexism and homophobia?

12. What are your physical, intellectual, and emotional abilities? What is your experience related to those abilities and/or disabilities?

13. Do you have any physical characteristics that cause people to notice you? Has this been positive or negative? What about you makes you unnoticeable? Has this been positive or negative?

Based on this analysis:

- On what levels have you experienced other peoples' ignorance? Stereotyping?

- On what levels have you experienced prejudice? Exhibited prejudice?

- On what levels have you experienced discrimination? Exhibited discrimination?

- On what levels have you experienced institutionalized oppression?

- In what ways are you a member of the dominant group(s) and in what ways are you a member of minority groups?

- What aspects of your own culture and sources of internalized oppression provide avenues for you to find commonalities with those who are different from you?

____

____

____

____

____

____

- In what ways are you better able to understand human similarities and differences?

____

____

____

____

____

____

Critical-Thinking Activity D

Self-Awareness and Race

This activity is intended to focus on issues of racism in your field placement or place of employment. The goal is to help you assess how self-awareness in your professional role(s) affects your minority clients.

Start by listing all the roles you are currently playing in your organization (for example, case manager, clinician, advocate, data manager/researcher, community organizer, supervisor, and so on):

____

____

____

____

____

____

For each role, ask yourself the following questions:

1. What happens when I am with someone of another color, race, or ethnicity?
2. What is my level of acceptance? (Do I look for common bonds with people who are different from me? What do I do?)
3. What are my attitudes toward or about minorities? (Do I stereotype people who are different from me? Are there any groups in particular that are problematic for me?)
4. How broad is my knowledge base?
5. How do I use my knowledge to help minority clients?
6. What is my response when I am identified as contributing to racism?
7. Can I detect or delineate differences in my transactions with minority clients? Colleagues?

Use the grid that follows to respond to each question, according to role. After completing the grid, analyze your responses to determine if there are themes that suggest that changes might be warranted. If there are themes, develop a plan of action for change.

Self-Awareness Grid

	Role #1	Role #2	Role #3	Role #4
1. What happens when I am with someone of another color, race, or ethnicity?				
2. What is my level of acceptance?				
3. What are my attitudes toward or about minorities?				
4. How broad is my knowledge base?				

Self-Awareness Grid (*continued*)

	Role #1	Role #2	Role #3	Role #4
5. How do I use my knowledge to help minority clients?				
6. What is my response when I am identified as contributing to racism?				
7. Can I detect or delineate differences in my transactions with minority clients? Colleagues?				

Critical-Thinking Activity E

A Continuum of Awareness

M. E. Kondrat (1999)[2] identified five types of self-awareness and Netting and O'Connor (2003)[3] expanded on them. Look at each type listed below:

- **Preconscious Awareness**
  One begins to realize that he or she is not self-aware.
- **Simple Conscious Awareness**
  For the first time, one experiences awareness.
- **Reflective Awareness**
  One thinks about and reflects on what has happened in simple conscious awareness.
- **Reflexive Awareness**
  One pays particular attention to and understands how personal history and one's personhood affect the situation.
- **Social Constructive Awareness**
  One recognizes the mutual meaning-making that shapes what has happened in a situation.
- **Critical Reflectivity**
  One accepts responsibility for the role she or he played in the situation and asks questions about biases and power dynamics in the situation.
- **Contextual Awareness**
  One recognizes how raising questions about biases and power affect others, seeing the self in context.

Having read these definitions, see if you can provide an example of when you used each type of awareness. If you have not experienced a particular type, make a plan to go to that level of awareness. Think about the costs and benefits of each level of awareness.

[2]Kondrat, M. E. (1999). Who is the "self" in self-aware: Professional self-awareness from a critical theory perspective. *Social Service Review, 73,* 451–477.

[3]Netting, F. E., & O'Connor, M. K. (2003). *Organization practice: A social worker's guide to understanding human services.* Boston: Allyn & Bacon.

Critical-Thinking Activity F

Complex Thinking

Kroeger and Thuesen (1988)[4] have identified five levels of complex thinking along a hierarchy beginning with simply copying and moving toward synthesis.

- **Copying**
  Writing down what happens verbatim.

- **Comparing**
  Looking at what occurred at one time as compared to what happened in another situation. Possibly comparing two reports or studies.

- **Computing**
  Tabulating data from the comparison.

- **Analyzing**
  Drawing conclusions about the differences or similarities that you have compared.

- **Coordinating**
  Sharing what has been learned in the analysis process with decision makers.

- **Synthesizing**
  Moving from concrete information to examining the implications of what has been compared.

Looking at the definitions above, identify when you have engaged in each level of thinking for information management. What purpose do you think each level serves and what are the problems with each level of information management?

[4]Kroeger, O., & Thuesen, J. M. (1988). *Type talk.* New York: Dell.

Critical-Thinking Activity G

Planning for Personal and Professional Safety

Talk with your supervisor in your field agency or place of employment and ask for the employee safety plan. Look for instructions regarding:

- Safety within the office
- Car/travel safety
- Safety in the community

1. Analyze the procedures for thoroughness. Is there sufficient detail for you to know precisely what you should do to protect yourself? To protect your colleagues? To protect your clients?

2. If details are missing, make recommendations about what should be included. Include a plan for how you would assure that the changes are accepted.

3. If there is no safety plan, develop one that covers, at a minimum, office, travel, and community safety. Are there other elements that should also be considered?

4. Share your ideas with members of your class who are associated with similar agencies. Build yours from the ideas of the others. How might you assure that your agency adopts a safety plan?

Part 2

Policy Practice

Keywords:

change
formal
informal
large systems
macro practice
policy
policy advocacy
policy practice
policy-related activities
policy sensitivity

Introduction

Given the importance of policy in the social work profession, we begin our focus on macro practice at the policy level. We see policy as a gateway to all levels of macro practice.

We recognize that the word "policy" can be intimidating because you may not see yourself as a policy expert. Let us reassure you that you may know more about policy than you suspect. You have probably already had much experience, direct or indirect, with policy. If you are renting an apartment, there are policies that protect you as a renter. If you are buying groceries, there are policies that dictate what can be sold under what conditions so that you will not become ill. If you are applying for a driver's license, there are policies that dictate under what conditions you can obtain one.

Policies, in the most general sense, can be defined as directives that guide actions. Therefore, policies may be informal and not written down. For example, if the staff in an agency agree that only they can use the copy machine, then someone not on staff may be told "it's our policy that only staff use this equipment." This is a directive, developed by the employees in an office or organization, that guides action (who can use the machine). On a higher level, if a state legislature approves a policy, and it is signed into law by the governor, that any professional who is aware of child abuse must report it, then the directive requires a professional to take action when abuse is apparent. It is policy and it is part of state law. It is mandatory and there may be penalties if one does not follow the policy. Policies, therefore, can be informal or highly formalized. They guide our actions in arenas in which we work and live.

Policy therefore influences not only what is possible at all levels of large-system practice, but also in direct practice with individuals or groups. In this section of the workbook we will look at the complex arena of policy to help you gain a comfort level and a degree of competence in policy work.

There are different kinds of competence in dealing with policy. Policy-sensitive practice means that a professional is aware of how policies influence people's lives and acts accordingly. For example, if you work with an older client who needs in-home services, you would be aware that home-care agencies are regulated and that certain tasks require professionals with various licenses. You would also be aware that some agencies accept Medicaid and others do not. If your client is on Medicaid, you would want to refer the client to an agency that will accept this type of payment. Being sensitive does not mean that you know all the ins and outs of Medicaid or home-health-care regulation, but rather that you know enough to make an appropriate referral in conjunction with your clients' needs and resources.

We begin this section based on our assumption that being policy sensitive is a professional social work responsibility. Exercises and activities listed in the policy practice chart under demystifying, conceptualizing and defining, and increasing sensitivity are intended to support policy-sensitive practice.

Social workers may be called upon to act beyond performing policy-sensitive practice and actually perform policy-related activities such as "brokerage, liaison, and advocate services [requiring] skills such as mediation and conflict management."[1] We want to be sure that you can go beyond policy sensitivity and engage in policy-related activities. Policy-related activities require you to be able to identify policies at various levels, analyze them using frameworks of analysis, and be capable of articulating how policy either impedes or enhances services and benefits for persons in need, regardless of client population or social concern.

In this section there are also opportunities to develop an understanding of policy practice and policy advocacy. Policy practice is defined as "efforts to change legislative, agency, and community settings, whether by establishing new policies, improving existing ones, or defeating policy initiatives of other people."[2] Policy advocacy is a form of policy practice "that aims to help relatively powerless groups such as women, children, poor people, African Americans, Asian Americans, Latinos, gay men and lesbians, and people with disabilities, improve their resources and opportunities."[3] Under the section on enhancing policy-change skills (the last section in the chart that follows) are exercises in planning for and establishing new policies, revising and improving existing policies, or opposing policy initiatives of others.

Because few students come to social work education with extensive policy experience, we have designed exercises and activities first to demystify policy—and the political process that undergirds social policy. We have also designed exercises that provide successively more complex experiences in order to expand analytic and practice skills to a larger, more public platform. Being comfortable in the role of a policy advocate, using assertive stances in politically charged environments, whether in the legislature, the community, or host agency, is our goal.

These exercises develop in the safety of the classroom, but we know that the activities may take students into the real world where policy changes actually occur. We assure you that these skills, when developed, have proven to be extremely effective beyond the classroom. Much of what we provide are examples of the tedious groundwork necessary to make change happen. At the conclusion of this section your policy-practice repertoire will include letters written to influence legislators, plans for lobbying, and skills in advocacy methods. Planfulness will be the key, because once any hesitancy about policy practice has been overcome, the adrenaline rush that accompanies the power of policy work may pull attention away from the basics of change agentry at the policy level. In the excitement of the process, it is important not to lose sight of why the change is needed and who will benefit as a result of that change.

"The Days of Our Placements: Scene III"

It did not take long for the student unit at Community House to engage the realities of practice. Within days of completing an on-site orientation to the agency, they found themselves confronted with a policy issue.

Maria told the other four students that she had learned that several elementary-aged children had been injured at home after school in the last six months. She had

---

[1]Jansson, B. (1999). *Becoming an effective policy advocate: From policy practice to social justice* (4th ed.). Pacific Grove, CA: Brooks/Cole. p. 55.

[2]Ibid., p. 13.

[3]Ibid.

previously worked with an EMS service to help pay for her undergraduate education and, while learning her way around the Community House neighborhood, had stopped at the local public-safety installation to chat with the EMS workers. She thought she might pick up a few tips about the neighborhood. Some of the EMS staff mentioned that one of their frustrations was that they often had to treat young children who suffered at-home accidents late in the afternoon—scalding, kitchen-knife cuts, poisoning, and falls—all of which were perfectly preventable if parental or adult supervision were present. However, many parents worked so children went unsupervised after school. Maria knew that records of the time of day of each call, the injury, and what the resolution was would be available, since she had once organized and kept these types of records when she worked with an EMS.

When Maria reported this situation to the others, Tamara said, "Let's check with our field instructor to see if anyone is doing anything about this. It is really too bad that this has to go on. Somebody has to be concerned for those children." They agreed and, upon inquiring, learned that there was an identified "latch-key children" problem in the neighborhood, and they were referred to the local newspaper, *The Daily,* to check its Internet archives for the previous year, when a series of stories had featured this problem, among others faced by the community. Yusof checked and then shared copies of the article with the others and, in addition, contacted the United Way Referral Service to see if after-school services or day care were available to children and families in the community. He learned that this was a "gap" in the service network for the neighborhood.

The group discussed this and met with the field instructor, proposing that something ought to be done, as children were suffering and no one was doing anything about it. When asked what should be done, Chrystal, who was very much enjoying the class they were all taking in social work practice with organizations and communities, quickly said, "Well, from what we are studying in class, it seems that since we have a description of the condition and have verifying data of a problem, we could develop some intervention options and goals to meet the problem." Harry, not one to sit back and let others get too far out in front, then added, "Right, one thing that could be done would be to get the school board to provide after-school programs in cooperation with the parks and recreation department. Remember in our social welfare history reading how using school buildings for community activity after school was tried way back in the early 1900s in Boston under the leadership of Mary Parker Follett?"

The other four just looked sideways at one another, thinking, there he goes again, off into his own world. Their field instructor, not wanting the opportunity to teach pass unused said, "Well, that is one possibility. Are there others—especially others that might do something for the kids right now, since school board action would be a good long range possibility?" "Well, speaking of history, I recall that early settlement houses ran after-school programs for kids, combining recreation and education," added Tamara. "This agency was a settlement house; why not return to its roots and run an after-school program here?" Harry, who really identified with the settlement movement, jumped in again by pointing out that settlement work also involved parent education about child rearing, and he suggested a parent-education program be initiated. Pleased with the commitment to the matter and the children, the field instructor summarized their options and then posed a challenge. "You know, you are really policy sensitive in your thinking, and you have identified longer-range policy-practice issues at the community level with the schools. You have also identified agency policy matters in terms of agency programming and resources, and you seem to be acting as advocates for the children. I would like to challenge you, as a team, to grapple with how to be effective on this matter on behalf of the children. What are the change priorities going to be? What is best for the children? I'd like to see you take this on, in addition to the individual assignments you all have. Do you want to do it?"

Policy Practice: Exercise and Activity Chart

Focus	Exercises	Activities
Demystifying Policy	Exercise 1: Policy Issues Exercise 2: Faith and Government Exercise 3: Alzheimer's Volunteers Exercise 4: Policy Levels	Activity A: Political Cartoons Activity B: Policy-Presentation Guide
Conceptualizing and Defining Policy	Exercise 5: Policy-Practice Definitions Exercise 6: Policy Options	Activity C: Federal Law Activity D: White-Paper Analysis Activity E: Policy Language
Increasing Policy Sensitivity	Exercise 7: Policy-Implementation Options Exercise 8: The Tattoo Bill Exercise 9: Sensitivity Chart	Activity F: Policy Intent
Practicing Policy-Related Tasks	Exercise 10: Lobbying Knowledge Checklist	Activity G: Policy Sources
Enhancing Policy-Change Skills	Exercise 11: Gun-Control Advocates Exercise 12: Policy-Analysis Model	Activity H: Rational/Nonrational Activity I: Gun Control

Policy-Practice Exercises

Policy-Practice Exercise 1

Policy Issues: Identifying Disagreements

If an issue has been raised, it means that there is disagreement, and there are many disagreements over social policies. If an issue is being discussed, it means that someone has determined that there is a problem to be solved. Many things can affect what policy is developed—even the way an issue is phrased. The intent of this exercise is to examine just how many different "issues" emerge in examining any policy.

Step 1: Identify a social policy at the national or state level. Write a brief statement, indicating the problem this policy addresses.

Step 2: Answer each of the following questions:

- What do you think are the major issues surrounding this policy?

- What are the issues about how the policy is worded?

- Who are the people, groups, and organizations particularly interested in these issues and why are they interested?

- What are the issues about who the policy affects?

- Who has the power to address these issues?

- What are the chances that these issues will be resolved?

- Do you have an opinion about the issues you have identified?

Step 3: Decide whether you think this policy should be kept "as is," should be revised in some way, or should not be approved. When you have decided, take five minutes to persuade the class about your views.

Policy-Practice Exercise 2

Faith and Government

You have just opened the local newspaper and you read the following story:

WHAT'S FAITH GOT TO DO WITH IT?

A few years ago, well-known evangelist Farley Smith denounced the presidential administration's push for a faith-based initiative, warning that such an effort would make legitimate religious charities dependent on government. His exact words had been, "Religious groups will become government prostitutes, no longer independent or able to speak their minds." Today, Search for Truth International, a charity established by Smith in 1995, will receive federal dollars provided to religious organizations to provide social services.

Last January on the nationally televised talk show Smith hosts once a week, he proclaimed the demise of the charitable religious sector if it succumbs to public dollars. His exact words were: "The wrath of God himself will come down on our heads if we join forces with government, and the separation of Church and State will fade into oblivion. Government dollars are tainted dollars. They are the narcotic for the soul of freedom and will immobilize us into complacency." Asked if Smith had changed his view of faith-based programs, sources told us that "he is out of town and has no comment at this time."

The faith-based measures originally instigated by the Administration have been the source of criticism from liberals and conservatives alike. Liberals have railed against the intent to blur lines between church and state, whereas conservatives have been fearful that public dollars will reduce their ability to evangelize, undercutting the integrity of their religious mission.

Use the newspaper story above as a stepping-off point to discuss the following questions:

1. How do you feel about the news story above? What is your "gut reaction"?

____

____

____

____

2. How would you define the terms *faith* and *faith-based*?

____

____

____

____

3. Why do you think there is such controversy over faith-based initiatives?

4. Do you think that faith-based service provision is different from secular service provision? Why or why not?

5. Why are there concerns about the separation of church and state in the faith-based initiative movement?

6. What are the implications of providing faith-based services for clients? Does it matter?

Policy-Practice Exercise 3

Alzheimer's Volunteers: An Agency Policy Simulation

For this exercise, select ten people to role-play that they are members of a board of directors. Each person should introduce themselves and the role they are assuming. The roles follow:

- An M.S.W. social worker who directs the Area Agency on Aging, a planning agency for the planning and service area in which the Alzheimer's Association is located.
- A B.S.W. social worker who is employed by a local for-profit nursing home.
- A clergy person who is the chaplain at a local faith-based retirement community.
- A nurse who has expertise in end-of-life care and works for a local palliative-care unit at the hospital.
- A banker from a large national organization, located at a branch in this town.
- A lawyer who has a large geriatric practice in the area.
- A social work educator who teaches in the School of Social Work.
- A geriatrician–physician who teaches in the Medical School.
- An older person who represents consumers.
- A manager for a local home-health organization.

The Alzheimer's Association has formed a local chapter in your community. It has gained nonprofit status. You have been asked to serve as members of the newly formed board of directors. Various chapters around the country have made available their policies-and-procedures manuals. However, you need to formulate a number of policies that are specific to your local organization. The subject of this board meeting is focused on one such policy.

A proposed policy statement has come to the board. It reads as follows:

> This Alzheimer's Association chapter will use numerous volunteers to staff support groups throughout the area. It is our intent to provide the highest-quality volunteer program. In order to do this, all volunteers will be carefully screened and selected. The screening process will include criminal background checks, the submission of at least three references, the completion of an application form, a personal interview with the Executive Director, mandatory training, continuing education, and a three-month probationary period.

As board members read this statement there are raised eyebrows. One board member says, "Well, we're all volunteers and I think this reads more like we're hiring people than recruiting volunteers. This sounds way too bureaucratic to me."

Another responds, "But, we're liable if anything goes wrong and these volunteers will have direct contact with caregivers. Besides, we want to weed out anyone who can't do the best possible job."

"But wait . . . ", another voice is heard, "Who will even do all this work? It takes time to follow through on background checks, to do interviews, to provide training, etc. etc. We only have an executive director and a part-time secretary. Who is going to do all this?"

As the meeting continues, dialogue becomes heated as the board struggles with a multitude of concerns.

Role Play Directions

Role-play a dialogue about what you see as the implications of this proposed policy for the staff, board, and volunteers of this organization.

Class members not participating in the role-play should observe.

Following the role-play, debrief using these questions:

1. What policy issues emerged in this process?
2. Did people from different disciplines respond with different perspectives?
3. What was the resolution? Was the policy statement amended and why?
4. What was observed about group dynamics in this process and what can be learned from these observations?
5. Did the observers agree with the assessment of the role-play participants? If not, what might account for the difference?

Policy-Practice Exercise 4

Policy Levels: From the Personal to the National

These activities are designed to help you see where policies operate and what their consequences tend to be.

1. Write down a personal policy. This should be a policy that guides you in your own life (for example, taking off your shoes at the front door). Determine the benefits and costs of this policy.

2. Identify a similar family policy that operates within your own family (for example, everyone visiting your house should take off their shoes at the front door). What are the costs and benefits of this policy?

3. Now identify an agency policy. This could be anything that guides the activities of an organization known to you (for example, workers have to wear certain types of shoes that meet certain standards). What costs and opportunities are created by this policy?

4. Describe a city or local policy, one that applies to those living in your specific community (for example, people must wear shoes in order to be served in any restaurant or eating establishment). What is gained and what is lost by this policy?

5. What would be an example of a state policy? Identify a policy that applies to the citizens of your state (for example, restaurants can only serve customers who wear shoes and shirts). Determine the costs and benefits of the policy.

____

____

____

6. Articulate a federal policy that applies to all those living within the United States (for example, manufacturers of shoes must be incorporated and abide by standards established for the shoe industry). What are the positive and negative consequences of this policy?

____

____

____

____

7. Using radio, television, or written media as a resource, find stories describing policies at the six levels identified above. Determine if any of the policies at one level have consequences at another level. Write in your comments below:

____

____

____

____

Policy-Practice Exercise 5

Policy-Practice Definitions

The following concepts are central to policy practice. Develop a thorough definition of each.

1. Social problem

____

____

2. Social need

____

____

3. Social policy

____

____

4. Social program

____

____

5. Social change

____

____

Now look at your definitions. Does the definition change when the concept is used at different stages in the policy process (policy development versus modification of existing policy)? For example, would you alter your definition if you were thinking about a policy that was just being developed, as opposed to analyzing one that was already in place?

Policy-Practice Exercise 6

Policy Options

This exercise is designed to be as flexible as possible—each group selects a topic of their choice. It is also designed to demonstrate various policy concepts.

First, choose a problem you would like to address. Discuss this to determine if it is something the group agrees is a problem and that the members of the group feel they know at least something about. Write a statement of the problem.

Second, talk about the problem. What are the history, theoretical perspectives, current research and practice findings, gender and ethnic considerations, and etiology of the problem? Knowing that you don't have access to the latest literature, draw from the expertise of the people within the group.

Third, discuss the following questions:

- What policy options can you identify that might be viewed as solutions to this problem?

- What criteria can you identify that should be used to compare and contrast these policy options?

____

____

____

____

- Develop a decision matrix that uses policy options and criteria. (Decide if you want to quantitatively rank these criteria or if you want to take a qualitative approach.)

____

____

____

____

Decide how your group will report on the process you have gone through. This will be informally done during a class debriefing period.

Policy-Practice Exercise 7

Policy-Implementation Options

Policies are courses of action that have implications for various target population groups. Below are a series of potential implications for people trying to implement policy intent.

Form small groups and debate how you would implement the requirements of the brief scenarios below.

1. Current law requires that any unwed mother who receives welfare must cooperate with the welfare department in naming and locating the father of her child. How would you implement this policy if you were caseworkers who strongly believed in this policy? Strongly opposed this policy?
2. Current welfare policies encourage maximum feasible self-sufficiency among the poor who receive services. What does this mean? How is this being implemented?
3. You practice in a state that requires that anyone convicted of sexual abuse be registered by the state, and upon release from prison that the community in which this person chooses to live must be notified of the offender's status as a convicted sexual offender. How do you implement this?
4. One state is beginning to develop an automated eligibility system. Under this system the caseworker will input the information about the family into the computer and the computer will determine if the family is eligible and how much the grant would be. What implementation problems do you think will arise when this system is installed in welfare offices?
5. You work for a small nonprofit social service agency that has just received a mandate to have at least one bilingual social worker on staff to obtain continued funding. You currently have none. What implementation issues does this raise?
6. You are a medical social worker who has been asked to be the organ transplant designee for the hospital. This, according to state law, means that you are required to approach any patient who is dying to determine if they are willing to be an organ donor. What implementation issues does this raise?
7. Assume that there is a university-wide policy that requires all graduate students to be administered a comprehensive examination. You are a student in the School of Social Work, and that school's response to the mandate is an oral comprehensive examination administered during the last semester of your tenure at the university. Given that the university-wide policy does not specify method of administration, what implementation options do you see available to the school?

Policy-Practice Exercise 8

The Tattoo Bill: Regulating Tattoo Parlors and Body-Piercing Salons

You are a group of concerned citizens who want to have tattoo parlors and body-piercing salons regulated. A bill has been introduced in the legislature to address this. However, you also know that it sometimes takes years for policy options to get through any legislative session and you are determined to keep this issue on the public agenda. Discuss the following questions and come up with a strategy for how you will influence change.

1. How would you frame the problem statement, given the content of the current bill (see pp. 78–79) and what you know about these issues?

____

____

2. Would you have a different statement of the problem for different target groups? If so, how would those statements differ?

____

____

3. Why are definitions so important here?

____

____

4. Do the definitions in the proposed bill seem on target, or would you change them?

____

____

5. What are the policy options here?

____

____

6. Can you come up with an alternative proposal that would stand a chance of being passed?

____

____

____

7. What would be the important factors to consider in drafting an alternative?

____

____

8. How would you keep this issue on the political agenda?

____

____

9. What would be the challenges in keeping this on the agenda? Are there advocacy groups who could help you?

____

____

10. Write a brief proposal for what you would like to have happen. Then critique the current proposed bill in terms of trade-offs (advantages and disadvantages).

____

____

____

HOUSE BILL NO. 683

Offered January 10, 2005

Prefiled January 9, 2005

A BILL to amend and reenact § 35.1-503 of the Code of the State, to amend by adding in Chapter 4 of Title 35.1 a section numbered 35.1-505, and to repeal § 13.1-234 of the Code of the State, relating to regulation of tattoo parlors

Patron — Jones

Referred to Committee on Health, Welfare, and Institutions

Be it enacted by the Legislative Assembly:

That § *35.1-503* of the Code of this State is amended and reenacted, and that the Doe is amended by adding in Chapter 4 of Title 35.1, a section numbered *35.1-505* as follows:

§ 35.1-503. Inspections.

Inspectors of the State Bureau of Health may inspect each barbershop, cosmetology salon, nail care salon, *tattoo parlor,* and *body-piercing salon* in the State on a regular basis. Any infractions shall be immediately reported to the Bureau of Health and the Director of Occupational and Professional Regulation for disciplinary action. The Board may inspect barbershops, barber schools, cosmetology salons and schools, and nail care salons and schools, *tattoo parlors,* and *body-piercing salons* for compliance with regulations promulgated by the Board.

§ 35.1-505. Regulation of tattoo parlors and body-piercing salons; definition; exception.

A. Except as provided in this section, no person shall engage in the operation of a tattoo parlor or body-piercing salon without the Board having issued a valid registration.

B. By regulation, the Board shall establish requirements for regulating any tattoo parlor or body-piercing salon and shall specify protocols for enforcing compliance with the disease control and disclosure requirements of § 19.1-553.4, including unannounced inspections by certified personnel. The Board may regulate the sanitary conditions of personnel, equipment, and premises of tattoo parlors and body-piercing salons.

C. For the purposes of this section:

"Body-piercing salon" means any location in which the act of penetrating the skin to make a hole, mark, or scar, generally permanent in nature, is performed. "Body piercing" does not include the use of a mechanized, pre-sterilized ear-piercing system that is used to place a hole in the lobe or outer perimeter of the ear.

"Tattoo parlor" means any place in which designs, letters, scrolls, figures, symbols, or any other marks are placed upon the skin of any person in ink or in any other substance, resulting in permanent skin coloration. This includes permanent makeup or permanent jewelry by the aid of needles or any other instrument that touches or punctures the skin.

D. This section shall not apply to medical doctors, veterinarians, registered nurses or any other medical services personnel licensed to Subtitle II of this title in performance of their professional duties.

Policy-Practice Exercise 9

Sensitivity Chart: A Tool for Analyzing Policy

You are a team of social workers employed in a large public bureaucracy. Your supervisor has just asked you to assist in an important task that needs to be completed today. This large public agency constantly is reviewing bills that are being proposed in the state legislature. Often, skilled policy analysts are hired to look over certain bills that may affect the agency, its clients, or the community in which the agency is located, and to consult with agency staff about the implications.

However, your supervisor has often felt less than fully comfortable with the results, as they do not focus in a usable and systematic way on the needs of the agency's clients, many of whom are women and members of minority groups. As the supervisor says, "The policy-analysis models used are just not designed to get to concerns of gender, race, and ethnicity." Instead of traditional analysis models, the following chart is suggested as a framework you can apply to policy proposals.

Select a policy with which you are familiar and practice using the chart that follows. In each box put either "yes," "no," or "NA" (not applicable). Be prepared to talk about the implications of what you have learned by using this process. Make notes about these implications in the following space.

Policy-Sensitivity Chart

Men	Women	Racial Groups	Ethnic Groups	Sexual Minorities	Persons with Disabilities	Elders	Questions to Keep in Mind when Reviewing Bills
							To which groups is the language in this policy sensitive?
							Which of these populations have access to the services/ opportunities mentioned in this policy?
							Does this policy account for different cultural perspectives?
							Is this policy hostile or indifferent to any of these population groups?
							Does this policy take into account varying opportunities available to these population groups?

Policy-Practice Exercise 10

Lobbying Knowledge Checklist

Please check the items that best describe your lobbying experience. Be prepared to discuss in class those experiences you have had and how you would add experiences you have not had.

________ I am aware of the general election day in my state (month ___ and day___).

________ I know the names of my senators in the U.S. Senate.

____

____

________ I know the name of my representative in the U.S. House of Representatives.

____

________ I know my senator in the Senate (or Assembly) of my state.

____

________ I know my representative in the House (or Assembly) of my state.

____

________ I know my local government (city, village, county, township, town) elected representative.

____

________ I know about the legislative process, but I have never participated in lobbying activities.

________ I know about the legislative process, and I have participated in lobbying activities.

For example: ____

________ I have spoken with at least one of my local, state, or federal elected representatives regarding a policy issue important to clients of social workers, to social service programs, or to citizens in general.

Policy-Practice Exercise 11

Gun-Control Advocates: Staying on the Public Agenda

You belong to a group of concerned citizens who want to support gun-control legislation. Recently, your state legislature has failed to support gun-control measures. You realize that the likelihood of legislation being passed during the current session is slim, and you are disappointed. Several members of your group have experienced the death of friends or acquaintances due to unregulated gun ownership and use. However, you know that it can take years for policy options to get through the legislature and you are determined to keep this issue on the public agenda. Discuss the following questions and come up with a plan for how you will pursue this.

1. How would you keep your concerns on the public agenda?

2. What would be the challenges of doing so?

3. Are there advocacy groups who could help you?

4. How would you frame the problem statement, given what you know about gun-control issues?

5. Would you have a different statement of the problem for different target audiences? If so, in what respect would those statements differ?

6. Can you come up with a plan that will keep the public and legislators informed and aware of the issue?

7. What would be the important factors to consider in developing your plan?

8. Write a brief plan for what you would like to have happen.

9. Finally, critique your proposal in terms of trade-offs (advantages and disadvantages).

Come back to class ready to discuss your plans.

Policy-Practice Exercise 12

Policy-Analysis Model: Developing One's Own

Develop your own framework to analyze social policy. In doing so, consider the values of the profession according to the National Association of Social Workers' Code of Ethics, which says, in summary, that social workers should:

- Have as a primary goal helping people in need and addressing social problems
- Challenge social injustice
- Respect the inherent dignity and worth of the person
- Recognize the central importance of human relationships
- Behave in a trustworthy manner
- Practice within their areas of competence and develop and enhance their professional expertise

What elements should go into your policy-analysis model that would allow you to test a policy according to these values?

Be sure that your model, at a minimum, addresses the following:

- Allows a description of a problem situation
- Specifies criteria for making choices between alternatives
- Generates alternatives
- Allows the selection of the "best" solution
- Allows assessment of feasibility regarding policy selection, implementation, and experience

Be prepared to explain the rationale for your model to the class.

Policy-Practice Activities

Policy-Practice Activity A

Political Cartoons

Go to the cartoon page in your local newspaper and locate a cartoon that reflects a policy issue. Remember that cartoons often comment on the nature of relationships and societal issues. Humor, and even satire, are used to touch a chord in the reader and to put a different face on what are often serious issues.

Bring a cartoon that reflects a policy issue of any type to class. Be prepared to talk about the policy issue this cartoon portrays.

Next, go to the editorial page of your local newspaper and locate a political cartoon.

- What issues does this cartoon reflect?

____

____

____

- What political ideology seems to be guiding the cartoonist?

____

____

____

- How does it affect you?

____

____

____

Bring the editorial cartoon to class, and talk about why cartoons are used on editorial pages.

- What does a graphic or picture do that words cannot do?

____

____

____

Policy-Practice Activity B

Policy-Presentation Guide

This is a group activity that focuses on demystifying the concept of policy. As a group, you will prepare a classroom presentation. Begin by locating an article about a policy at any level of government (city, county, state, national) in your local newspaper that sparks your interest. Use whatever resources you wish to find information about this policy, including but not limited to additional reading, interviewing policy analysts, practitioners, recipients of service, and so on.

As a group prepare at least a 30-minute presentation and be prepared to respond to 15 minutes of questions from other class members. At a minimum, the presentation should cover:

Need Domain

1. Based on your readings, other preparation, and the analysis by the group, what is the need and the social problem related to this unmet need?
2. To define the problem, how are you and others using symbols, numbers, causes, interests, and decisions?
3. Based on this discussion, what are the primary policy issues and subissues your group wishes to address?

The Policy's Developmental Process or History

4. What is the existing policy?
5. Are there other relevant policy sources?
6. In what context was the policy derived?
7. What are the historical and ideological bases?
8. What value, economic, political, and other factors influenced the development of existing policy?
9. Were there significant leaders (political and/or expert) shaping the policy?

Policy Goals

10. Among the goals of equity, efficiency, security, and liberty, which goal was paramount during policy shaping? Policy implementing?
11. Is there any evidence of policy paradoxes (contradictions in policy results)?

Policy Solutions

12. What are the primary policy solutions now—Inducements? Rules? Facts? Rights? Powers?
13. How do the solutions relate or fail to relate to the current policy goals?
14. What are the positive and/or negative effects on the targeted population?

Policy Alternatives

15. What policy alternatives to the present policy are being considered?
16. If there are alternatives, what changes in goals, problem definition, and solutions seem to be evolving?

17. What is the group's assessment of the possibility that change to a policy alternative will occur?
18. If the change does occur, what will be the advantages and limitations for the targeted population?

Professional Response

19. Given your current assessment of the policy context, what would an appropriate social work role be in the current policy discourse?
20. What are your professional recommendations for the future of the policy?

When you present the policy, please provide the class with whatever materials would be helpful in understanding the complexity of the policy issue. At a minimum, this should include a list of the three best references used by your group. Remember, this is an exercise that should demonstrate an in-depth knowledge about a policy and a capacity to examine critically the effects of policy for clients, especially those in one's field agency. A further challenge is to participate persuasively in a political discourse to shape the perspectives and judgments of the classroom microcosm of the larger "polis."

Policy-Practice Activity C

Federal Law

Select one of the federal laws listed below. Obtain a copy of the law you have chosen and review it carefully.

1. Family Preservation and Support Services Program of the Omnibus Reconciliation Act 1993
2. P.L. 100-485, Income Security Social Security and Family Support Act of 1988
3. P.L. 100-294 Child Abuse Prevention, Adoption and Family Services Act of 1988 (If you prefer, you may use CAPTA or CAPTARA to illustrate your position.)
4. P.L. 96-272, Adoption Assistance and Child Welfare Act (AACWA) of 1980
5. P.L. 95-608, Indian Child Welfare Act of 1978
6. P.L. 94-142 Education for all Handicapped Children's Act of 1975 (If you prefer you may use the Amendments of 1986 [P.L. 99-457] or 1990 [P.L. 101-476] to illustrate your position.)
7. P.L. 93-415 Juvenile Justice and Delinquency Prevention Act of 1974
8. Adoption and Safe Families Act (SFA) of 1997
9. Multiethnic Placement Act (MEPA) of 1994

- What values are reflected in the law you reviewed?

___

___

___

- What impact does this law have on women, children, and minorities?

___

___

___

Policy-Practice Activity D

White-Paper Analysis

A White Paper, in the British tradition, is the culmination of an extensive analysis of a policy based on in-depth knowledge about the social problem for which a policy is being proposed. In the United States, a White Paper may go by various names, such as policy brief or study report. It is designed to be the result of a thorough investigation of the effects of policy on those suffering from the social problem addressed by the policy.

A White Paper is initially constructed from library research about the problem, its cause, and the policy solution. Identifying the problem and its potential solutions may result from interviews with experts, practitioners, and recipients of the service(s) designed to address the need or problem under investigation, and the analysis usually includes a variety of inputs from policy analysts. The White Paper is designed to give decision makers sufficient information to take a position regarding the need or problem domain and the current status of policy.

The following is an activity in research and analysis.

Step 1: Locate a White Paper. This could be a British White Paper, on child abuse for example, or it could be a position paper produced by a legislative research organization, a think tank, or an advocacy organization.

Provide a full citation, including title and date of publication.

____

____

Step 2: Look closely at the language used to describe the problem, those suffering from the problem, and the desired solution. Be sure to note the language related to the desired results of policy implementation. List the key words that give you clues about how the issues are constructed.

____________________	____________________
____________________	____________________
____________________	____________________
____________________	____________________

Step 3: Try to determine who funded the work necessary to produce the position paper. Are the authors listed? Who wrote it?

____

Is the association with either the funding or the producing organization clear?

____

Step 4: Based on Steps 1–3, describe the aims of the White Paper. What ideology or values perspective can you identify?

____

____

____

How does this point of view correspond or diverge from your personal and professional positions?

____

____

____

____

____

____

Policy-Practice Activity E

Policy Language

The following are a series of activities that may be used together to build a class dictionary, or can be used individually to demonstrate the importance of language nuance in policy practice.

1. Select a newspaper that covers legislative news. (This must be a major national or local paper that has a political section or that consistently covers state and federal legislative developments.) Using several articles, identify at least five acronyms.

2. From the articles, or based on further library research, find definitions for the acronyms. Through further research, determine where the acronyms fit organizationally in federal and state government. (This connection will most likely be to specific administrative offices, but it could be to advocacy or other entities that influence the governmental process.) What political implications do you see in either the words that make up the acronyms or the connections you have identified?

Acronym	Federal/State Government	Implications

3. From the Web or using other resources, locate your (or any available) state's legislative glossary. Analyze the glossary for policy jargon, rhetoric, and legalese. Change the definitions so that they are clearer and understandable by someone with a tenth-grade education. Compare the new definitions with the old. What are the consequences of the change?

4. As a team create your own dictionary of policy terms. Try to have at least 30 terms that range from policy identification through implementation to analysis and advocacy. Share your definitions with others in class. What are the consequences of the differences you discover?

____

____

____

Policy-Practice Activity F

Policy Intent: Challenges and Issues in Implementation

Locate a state-level policy that is either in the proposal stage or that has been enacted recently. Obtain a copy of the policy so that you can use it as a reference as you do this activity.

1. Write 1–2 sentences that succinctly state what problem this policy is intended to address.

2. What are the issues surrounding this policy? (Continue on a separate piece of paper if needed.)

3. Who are the key players in the governmental setting and/or relevant units that are, or will be, affected by this policy?

4. What population group(s) is targeted by this policy?

5. How do you think this policy came to be on the public agenda?

6. Why do you think certain solutions are proposed?

7. What are the political developments that may have shaped receptivity to the proposed policy?

8. Summarize what may be major challenges and issues in advocating for or against this policy.

Policy-Practice Activity G

Policy Sources

Select a specific service population, such as children and youth, families, the homeless, or elders. Based on your knowledge of the particular population:

1. Describe the major dimensions of the service system(s) that affect the needs of the population.

2. Identify the major sources of policy that shape service to the population.

3. Describe the policies' effects on direct social work practice or social work planning and administration.

4. Suggest some roles for social work in formulating, implementing, evaluating, or changing the policies in order to improve the service system or the programs serving the selected population in need.

5. What steps might you undertake to more thoroughly understand the policies and their impacts?

6. What would be the first step in policy analysis in order to give you sufficient information to act?

Policy-Practice Activity H

Rational/Nonrational: Comparison of Analysis Processes for Understanding Policy

There is more than one way to spin policy analysis. This activity will provide an example.

The Situation

Child Protective Services staff are experiencing much change and, as a result, feeling stress as their program is reorganized. There are 20 staff who are affected by the reorganization approved by the legislature and they need skills to help them address the needs of CPS clients. To serve clients well, it is important for staff to be prepared.

Analysis Processes

Two principal perspectives often shape policy analysis. Regardless of the details of the analytic process, they can be seen to be based on either rational or nonrational assumptions. Following is a comparison of the basic premises for each.

Rational	Nonrational
Single truth	Multiple, competing truths
Decisions made through series of well-defined steps	Decisions must include multiple understandings
Steps follow fixed sequence	No fixed sequence of analytic steps
Linear	Nonlinear
Based on market (biggest bang for the buck)	Based on power and politics
Most benefit, least cost	Context is everything
Based on objectivity and determinant rules	Decisions based on influence
Prediction based on objectives, alternatives, consequences	Getting what is "good" and avoiding what is "bad"
Decisions from selecting alternatives and minimizing objections	Making sense of paradox and politics
Reason as the basic building block	Reasoning by metaphor and analogy
Decisions made with assumptions of linearity	Decisions made with clarity and reason, but more fluid and circular
Experts dominate participation	Participation by all stakeholders
Policy-Analysis Types: • Rational • Chaotic • Garbage Can • Historic	**Policy-Analysis Types:** • Political • Contextual • Collaborative • Hermeneutic

Step 1: Think about the Child Protective Services situation stated above. Apply both the rational and non-rational approaches to the policy.

Step 2: Compare the results of analysis, particularly around the concept of social or distributive justice. What do you gain in amount of information available for decision making and what do you give up with each approach?

Policy-Practice Activity I

Gun Control

There are multiple ways in which you can express your views on policy matters. First, read the newspaper article at the end of this activity. Then choose one of the approaches provided below to express your views.

Writing Advocacy Letters

Compose a letter to the state legislator from your district urging continued legislative pursuit, consideration, and action on gun control. Remember to identify yourself and your relationship to the legislator, as well as any special knowledge base you have on the issue.

Preparing a News Release

Prepare a news release that will help keep this matter on the public agenda. Remember, you want the public to remain aware of this matter and would like continued legislative consideration. Remember to clearly indicate the name and reputation of the group you represent and to provide a contact person and directions for where to get additional information. News releases are of interest to the press only if the information contained in them is considered to be "newsworthy."

Persuading an Audience

Prepare comments to be presented at a public hearing on the issue and population it affects. First, inform yourself on the issue and the population. Second, identify and analyze the makeup of, and points of view of the potential audience. The following questions will help you do this:

1. Who are the major stakeholders (on all sides of the issue)?

___

2. Who is trying to persuade whom in the article?

___

3. What are the objectives of the people doing the persuading?

___

4. How would you evaluate and frame the audience that is being addressed in the article? Are there multiple audiences?

___

5. If you were going to take a stand about the problem, how would you begin?

   - What medium would you use?

___

- How would you sequence your presentations?

- What format might you use? (Speech, briefing, discussion, question and answer, other.)

- How would you rehearse and fine-tune your presentation?

ADVOCATES BLAST LEGISLATURE

Gun-control advocates yesterday blasted the state legislature for shooting down bills to promote gun safety and giving in to a powerful lobbying effort. Supporters of gun control pointed out that five related bills have been effectively killed for this session. They further claimed that bills prohibiting the government from suing gun manufacturers and distributors and banning local regulation of gun shows are moving through the assembly with ease, as if they were "shot from cannons."

"Legislators should be protecting our citizen's interests, not just the gun lobby," said Justine Trigerloc, President of Citizens Against Gun Violence, at a Capitol Hill news conference held by gun-control-advocacy organizations. In addition, a woman, whose 18-year-old daughter was fatally shot two years ago, blamed the actions on, "well-financed special-interest groups who hold us hostage almost at gunpoint until the legislature buckles to the gun lobby."

Statistics provided by Citizens Against Gun Violence showed that someone under 19 dies from gunfire nearly every three days in the state. Firearm injuries are cited as the second leading cause of death from unnatural causes among those 19 and under, according to the group.

To support their demands, gun-control supporters contended that the Speaker of the House of Representative's last campaign contribution report showed a $29,000 donation from the NRA last year. "This does not speak well to the state's ability to protect its youth, but it does speak to the condition of politics and legislative representation in our state," said B. J. Speakwel, Chairperson of Protect Our Youth, one of the cooperating organizations attending the news conference.

Part 3
Community Practice

Keywords:
change tactics and strategies
community assessment
community change
community development
community needs
community organizing
community planning
community-sensitive practice
community strengths
cultural competence
neighborhood
power

Introduction

In this section of the workbook, you will move closer to applied practice in and with communities. Having expanded our understanding of policy sensitivity and practice, we now turn to an important arena in which policy is implemented—the community. Themes we covered in the Policy Practice section are expanded upon as building blocks of contextual decision making. These themes are reflected in the chart that follows, in which exercises and activities are categorized according to whether they demystify community, help in conceptualizing or defining community, increase community sensitivity, provide opportunities to practice community-related tasks, or enhance community-change skills. Using these exercises and activities, we will clarify differences between community-sensitive practice, community planning, community organizing, and community development.

Practicing community sensitivity means that one has a basic understanding of and ability to analyze how communities do or do not meet human needs. In all the materials that follow, sensitivity will be a central theme. You will need to exercise cultural competence in order to engage in appropriately identifying both community resources and needs. Using good communication skills will be required in order to identify and engage with key indigenous community agents in formal or informal sectors in a community.

In this section you will develop understanding and analytical skills in macro practice through designing a community assessment that will include identifying community strengths and challenges. We will investigate the difficulties inherent in defining what constitutes a community or neighborhood, and will assess a community that includes not just geographical/political space, but also individual or familial space. This should help in understanding and articulating policy-driven multidimensional community needs and opportunities.

However, like policy-sensitive practice, community-sensitive practice is only a place to begin. Building on needs identification and assessment, the traditional problem-solving framework will be used to aid in designing plans for desired change. Planning requires looking ahead, thinking about all the possibilities, and being flexible enough to change one's approach as new information points toward a different direction. Community planning is a process that must be inclusive and social workers must consider ways to capture the voices of groups that are often not heard by persons in power. Therefore, exercises will guide you through participatory planning processes in which multiple voices are engaged.

Practicing sensitivity and planning are critically important, yet the work does not stop there. You must engage in change efforts in a community and evaluate the results of the efforts if policy is to be implemented at the local level. This requires you to do community organizing that mobilizes various individuals, groups, and organizations to support a change. This goes beyond hearing their voices; you must move toward action.

We will focus our attention on what happens through community-based social service agencies because they are most likely to stimulate and support professional community-change efforts by their social work employees, but we will also look at non–agency-based change, supporting the advocacy efforts students may choose to engage in without the sanction of an employing agency. Again, we will explicate multidimensional efforts in order to assure effectiveness at each stage of community change.

Community development is an ongoing process, with multiple episodes of planned change. We will illustrate this through a series of activities that provide opportunities to consider the use of different change strategies using multiple tactics. Community development has economic, political, and social aspects that require the professional social worker to think through a complex array of differences with the ultimate goal of community building.

Finally, this section will close with a look at power—its presence and use in participating in organizing change and development at the community level. We think a thorough look at the use and abuse of power is necessary in order to avoid naïveté in change actions. We will examine positive and negative uses of power, which are central to the identification and selection of appropriate change tactics and strategies within community settings.

"The Days of Our Placements: Scene IV"

Tackling the after-school needs of children proved to be complex. When they looked closely at the data, the students found that there were patterns that were easily discernable. The field instructor said that this indicated that there might be certain specific populations affected more than others and that perhaps it would be good to define the neighborhood more specifically, identifying the different communities that made up the area. Chrystal, in her polite, focused manner stated, "Why, this community has been here for years, for as long as I can remember. Everyone knows it is the working-class neighborhood of the city." "That may be true, but there must be reasons why it has always been known as the working-class neighborhood and has not lost that identifier," added Harry. The field instructor then said, "In fact, it does change in some ways, but some feel that it should maintain just one identity because it may be in their interest to have it so thought of." That set off Yusof, who blurted out, "Sure, the geography has not changed and it is still the Second Ward for local elections, but the present population sure looks different than the pictures from the 1930s that line the hallway leading to the director's office!" The field instructor expanded on this, agreeing that there have been changes, and asking the students to think about the different types of communities represented here. What are some of the types, or categories, of community? Are they represented in the Community House area? That might help identify target populations that would benefit from change and engage them in the change effort thorough some organizing work. She asked them to decide if they were undertaking the change effort "for" the community or "with" the community? That question really hit home with Maria, who said that it was the poorer families in which both parents worked, as well as one-parent families, that suffered due to a lack of after-school child care or programs. She pointed out that better-off families could have one parent at home at least for the after-school hours or pay for child care in another part of the city, while it was the poor who had no recourse to the "latch key." "To me, that seems unjust," added Tamara, and that led to a discussion of which of the intervention options might add an element of social and economic justice in the community. At the conclusion of the discussion, Chrystal, looking more concerned than anyone in the group had ever seen her, suggested that if they were really social workers, they should not, at a minimum, leave the powers that be unaware of the needs of these children who didn't have safe after-school environments.

Community Practice: Exercise and Activity Chart		
Focus	**Exercises**	**Activities**
Demystifying Community		Activity A: Community Encounter
Conceptualizing and Defining Community	Exercise 1: Community-Practice Definitions Exercise 2: What Is a Community? Exercise 3: Community-Service Assessment	Activity B: Geographical Community Assessment
Increasing Community Sensitivity	Exercise 4: LGBT Community Theater Exercise 5: Not in My Community	Activity C: The Barrio Landlord
Practicing Community-Related Tasks	Exercise 6: Outreach to Veterinarians Exercise 7: The Senior Center Exercise 8: Community-Relations Challenge	
Enhancing Community-Change Skills	Exercise 9: Promoting Community Dialogue Exercise 10: Central Hill Community Center Exercise 11: The Barrio Landlord	

Community-Practice Exercises

Community-Practice Exercise 1

Community-Practice Definitions

The following are important concepts, regardless of the community intervention one undertakes. Provide a full definition of each concept.

1. Community

2. Community organizing

3. Community functioning

4. Community building

5. Community development

6. Locality development

7. Social action

____

____

____

8. Social planning

____

____

____

Now determine if any of your definitions in 1–5 change depending upon whether you are engaging in change actions 6, 7, or 8.

Community-Practice Exercise 2

What Is a Community?

A functional (or dysfunctional) community can be: (1) a physical place, (2) a group with a common interest, or (3) an identity; geographically bounded like a neighborhood or bounded by the type of social or political organization.

What constitutes a community depends upon rules of inclusion and exclusion, such as:

- Physical barriers
- Political districts
- Ethnicity/culture
- Citizenship status
- Socioeconomic status
- Interests
- Collective identity
- Informal networks (relatives, friends, neighbors)
- Formal networks (institutions)

1. Individually, identify communities in which you hold membership. Then categorize them by place, or by a group with a common interest and/or identity (some may be both).

____

____

____

____

____

____

2. For each community identified, include what constitutes the rules of inclusion/exclusion for the community.

____

____

____

____

____

____

3. Now compare your results with those of your classmates. How do the similarities and differences affect resource availability in any of the communities identified?

Community-Practice Exercise 3

Community-Service Assessment

Create service-system groups by dividing the class into categories based on the type of placement or employment interest (for example, child welfare system, health system, mental health system, elder care system, and so on), then discuss the following questions. Be sure to record the important aspects of your discussion so that you can compare results of findings about one system with the others. Answer the following questions regarding your identified system.

1. How would you categorize target populations within the community? What are the major target populations within the system under discussion in your group? Is there a difference in perception of target populations between majority and minority community members?

____

____

____

____

____

____

2. If you were to prioritize aspects of the system's target population, which groups would rank as having the highest priority for services? Why?

____

____

____

____

____

____

3. Where would you go in this community to gather data about service needs of your target population?

____

____

____

____

____

____

4. What comprises the service system? Is it informal (provided by families, significant others, friends)? What are the formal dimensions (voluntary, private for-profit, public agencies)?

5. Ideally, what should the service delivery system look like? What should be the mix among the various aspects of the formal and informal systems?

6. What mechanisms should be in place to "glue" the system together? How would you assure that all components work as a system?

7. After comparing results among service system groups, what themes emerge? What does this mean for a viable community human-service system?

Community-Practice Exercise 4

LGBT Community Theater

The Laramie Project is a play that focuses on the story of Matthew Shepard, a young victim of a hate crime. In November 1998, ten people from New York traveled to Laramie, Wyoming to interview residents of that town about what happened to Matthew Shepard. The play they wrote after their visit focuses on the bigotry and tolerance, fear and courage, hate and hope that they discovered.

In your local community, the Lesbian, Gay, Bisexual and Transgendered (LGBT) Community Theater group is casting for *The Laramie Project,* which will be featured in their next season. Recent publicity in the local newspaper has sparked your interest in this play, but it has also made you aware of conflicts within the community. Read the newspaper article that follows and then answer these questions:

1. What are the issues raised in this newspaper article? Why are they so strongly felt?

2. If you were Jim Jamison, what would you do if you felt that your cast and crew might encounter resistance (or even be in danger)?

3. If you were Councilwoman Childs, what community strategies might you use to promote your view?

4. If you were the School Superintendent, what would you say when asked why you accepted money from the LGBT Community Theater group to purchase LGBT books and resources for your libraries?

5. Within this community, there is obvious tension. Is this tension the result of community values, history, social change, or other factors? Why do you think this tension exists?

6. What strategies and tactics might you use to promote communication between the LGBT community and persons who agree with Councilwoman Childs? Why might you want to promote communication?

____

____

____

LGBT THEATER GROUP ENCOUNTERS RESISTANCE

by Jane Moyer, Staff Reporter

"*The Laramie Project* is an incredible snapshot of what happens in today's society," says Jim Jamison. "It focuses on a community caught in the aftermath of a horrific event—the murder of a young man. And it makes us come face-to-face with the reality of our own thinking. How can it happen here in America? Can it happen in my own community? The play doesn't present just one view . . . it shows multiple views and multiple contradictions." Jamison is the director of the LGBT Theater Group and has just issued a casting call for the play.

Yet, *The Laramie Project* is only the tip of a glacier of controversy for the LGBT Theater. Their previous season featured a number of controversial productions. When they donated their profits to multiple causes, they came under fire. Proceeds from the season just ending have gone to the Gay, Lesbian, Straight Education Network to fund a billboard designed to raise consciousness about antigay harassment of LGBT youth in area schools; to the local school system to buy LGBT books and resources for their libraries; and to Meals on Wheels to underwrite the cost of meals for people with AIDS.

School Councilwoman Rhonda Childs says the theater group has gone too far. "It's okay that they want to raise consciousness for adults and produce plays with themes that promote their cause. Adults can choose whether to go to these plays. But then their proceeds are used to buy propaganda for our children in our public schools, and they have gone too far." Childs has been an outspoken critic, engaging in a public discourse with Jamison over a radio talk show several months ago.

In a recent interview, Jamison responded to Childs' criticisms. "It saddens me that Councilwoman Childs does not see the benefit in giving children knowledge in a safe environment. Raising awareness and promoting an atmosphere in which children can grow and develop to be the best they can be requires being open to their diverse identities." As for the donations, Jamison adds that any organization can donate to another, and "no one is refusing to take our money."

A call to the County Superintendent of Schools to determine if LGBT books and resources were actually being purchased, generated a "no comment."

Community-Practice Exercise 5

Not in My Community

A group that calls themselves "The Church of the Living Spirit" has approached the local library in your community for meeting space. The leader of the group explains that they are a nondenominational group with an expanding membership and that they try to meet in public space because they do not believe that "a church is a building." The local librarian schedules them to meet in the library's large conference room.

Two days later, notices appear in the local newspaper and fliers are posted in public areas around town. "The Church of the Living Spirit" is scheduled to meet at the community library on Saturday afternoon from 1:00-4:00.

You are curious about this group, so you go to their Web site to find out more about them. This is what you find:

> The Church of the Living Spirit is a social movement dedicated to purity. Our goal is to raise consciousness and awareness about the supremacy of certain human characteristics over others. We believe that all human beings can achieve a higher order of life, and that by recognizing those persons who are innately superior by nature of their race and gender, they can become leaders for others.

As you read on, you become more and more aware that this "movement" is what you would call a white supremacy group. The language about race throughout their Web site supports your assessment.

1. What would you do with this information?

___

___

___

2. Do you think that any group has the right to meet in the public library, regardless of their views? Are there certain views that are more controversial than others?

___

___

___

3. Would you consider attending the meeting? Why or why not?

___

___

___

4. Would you consider making a statement or taking an action? Why or why not?

___

___

___

5. Would you want to know what the local library's policy is concerning the use of its meeting space?

6. Do you think that this is a religious group? Why or why not?

7. Do you think there are different implications to this group meeting in a public library than meeting in their own building? Why or why not?

8. Would you react the same or differently in your role as a private citizen living in this community than you would in your role as a social worker? Explain your answer.

Community-Practice Exercise 6

Outreach to Veterinarians

The local animal league has been soliciting funds to build a "no-kill" shelter. A group of social work students are participating in the fund-raising effort and have joined forces with students from the School of Veterinary Medicine. When talking with students from the Vet School, you learn that there is going to be a community forum about the shelter and you decide to go.

At the community forum, the majority of people are there to support the new shelter. There are a few who don't want public dollars "drained for animals," but they are far outnumbered by passionate supporters. A number of animal lovers have actually brought their pets to the forum with them. It is an interesting mix of people and animals in a large meeting at the local senior center.

After the meeting, you are talking with two veterinarians who tell you that being at the senior center is making them a little anxious. They have a number of clients who attend the center and the veterinarians' practices seem to be heavily weighted toward older people with aging pets. One remarks, "If I have one more person come in and tell me that Muffy feels depressed, I don't know what I'll do." You ask what that means. "Oh," says the veterinarian, "it's very common for me and my colleagues to have older people come in to see us when they are feeling lonely. I give Muffy a placebo, but I know that the real reason they are there is because the owner is sad and isolated. And I don't know how to help people."

You know that there are number of resources in the community that help older people. You also know about resources in the mental-health community that deal with depression. It occurs to you that these groups and organizations often work with medical professionals as a matter of course, but you suspect they don't include veterinarians in their meetings and special events. It seems to you that it would be possible to link these community resources with the veterinarian community.

As a group, brainstorm what you might do about this situation.

Community-Practice Exercise 7

The Senior Center

A senior center offers a congregate meal and recreation program for elders. It is located in a community in which the elderly population (60 years and over) is 46 percent Hispanic and 54 percent Anglo. A group of Hispanic participants has approached the program director (an Anglo male) and identified a number of problems. Their concern is that the senior center reflects Anglo culture exclusively, offering little with which the Hispanic elderly can identify. The Hispanic participants are asking that culture be considered as a factor in planning meals; decorating the center; and celebration of holidays, activities, and programs. The director responds that he had never considered it, but welcomes their participation in redesigning the program and assigns you, the assistant program manager, to be the chair of a task force.

Please think through and report on the following questions:

1. In the above situation, who are the initiators of change, the clients who will benefit, the change agents, the targets of change, the planners, and the change implementers? (Remember, there is often overlap in these roles.)

   - Initiators of change

   ____

   ____

   - Clients who will benefit

   ____

   ____

   - Targets of change

   ____

   ____

   - Planners

   ____

   ____

   - Change implementers

   ____

   ____

2. Are there other major stakeholders? What perspective will be represented by each and how will each be involved, positively and negatively, in the change process?

Other stakeholders and their perspectives: ______________________________

____

____

____

3. How might the perspectives look if the director does not welcome bicultural programming?

4. What agency policies may need to be changed or developed to incorporate a new cultural perspective into program planning?

5. Who will be affected, positively and negatively? What will be provided? How will the policy be carried out? How will implementation be financed?

6. What might be the positive and negative unintended consequences?

7. How might the meal program be redesigned to incorporate cultural perspectives?

8. Assume that the director really does not welcome outside participation and has assigned you to keep this agitation contained. What position would be the most ethical, professional social work position to take? What would be your internal project design to achieve change within a year?

9. What steps, both internal and external, might the Hispanic participants undertake to solve this problem?

Community-Practice Exercise 8

Community-Relations Challenge

A group of concerned citizens in the Baptist church who wanted to address the needs of orphaned children founded a nonprofit agency in 1985. Originally a grassroots organization, it was run almost entirely by volunteers. As the agency grew and developed, and as times changed, it broadened its focus to include many children's services, obtained United Way funding, and gained a reputation for quality. In the last decade, it expanded rapidly as the public sector contracted with it to provide foster care, day care, and educational services to children and their parents. The agency opened two branch offices. During recent years the agency has moved away from it roots in the Baptist church, although it has never formally cut its ties to the church. The bylaws still require that at least 50% of the board be Baptist Church members. Today, funding consists of 60% government contracts, 20% United Way contributions, 5% government grants, 10% charitable contributions and fundraisers, and 5% Baptist fund drive.

The agency has a 16-member Board of Directors. There are twelve men and four women on the Board; one of the men is Native American and one man and one woman are African American. The Board usually trusts the administrator to provide oversight, to keep them up to date on impending issues and then to respond accordingly. They often refer affectionately to the agency as "the children's home"—a carryover from, and recognition of, the days when it was an orphanage.

In recent years, the agency has had to adapt to many changes in the environment and it is substantially different than when it was a "children's home." Eligibility guidelines have become stricter because of government constraints. Accountability to funding sources now requires careful evaluation of program outcomes. The agency has professionalized over the last twenty years, and employs M.S.W. and B.S.W. staff members. There used to be an active group of volunteers, but there are few today because there has not been time to recruit and train them. The administrator thinks it seems that the agency is losing touch with the community due to the demands it must meet from funding sources, and from not having time and resources to pay attention to volunteer needs and community relations.

The agency administrator came into the office this morning and found a letter that the agency receptionist said had been dropped off in person by its writer. After reading the letter, the administrator decides that this may be the catalyst that will move the staff to begin to reengage with the community. The staff is called together, including delivery and service supervisory staff, and charged with discussing how to respond to this situation and deciding if there are ways to make this apparent problem into an opportunity—an opportunity that might involve the letter writer, as well as other important constituents of the community.

As members of this staff group: (1) discuss the Director's charge, (2) prepare a report for presentation, and (3) analyze and comment on the process you went through as a group, including leadership, communication, and use of self.

The letter follows.

Mrs. Adrian Smith
35432 Tranquil Lane, Hometown, USA 53423

Today's Date

Administrator
Children's Services Agency
2003 Helping Drive
Hometown, USA

Dear Administrator:

I am writing to lodge a formal complaint against your agency. I also am prepared to take this situation to church authorities and the press if you ignore it.

Let me say first that I have been a strong supporter of your agency for many of my 75 years. In fact, I once was a volunteer with the Children's Home, and then I served for seven years as a board member. I have until recent years given money annually. The way things have been going for the Home, I have chosen not to contribute anymore, and after what I saw and heard yesterday, I am glad I made this decision.

Yesterday I saw one of your staff members on a television news program as she was speaking at a gay rights rally. She acknowledged at this public meeting that she is a lesbian. I was absolutely horrified to know that you would employ such a woman in an organization that serves young children.

This is not all! I understand from a friend who saw this news program with me that there may be other lesbian women at the agency. How could an agency of the church allow such people to become part of your staff?

As a former board member of your organization, I know that the people who represent the church on the board are not aware of this situation or they would have opposed the hiring of such persons. I hope you are prepared to take care of this situation immediately, and I will await your response.

Sincerely,
(Mrs.) Adrian Smith

Community-Practice Exercise 9

Promoting Community Dialogue

You've just attended a national conference that focused on "Creating Vibrant Communities" and you are excited about the possibilities you heard about. The conference was targeted at anyone interested in community work, particularly at the grassroots level. Conference organizers introduced a model program that promotes dialogue and reconciliation among racial groups, and you want to develop a similar program in your community. The goals of the national consciousness-raising model are these:

Direct and open communication: Initiating and sustaining dialogues with persons from every viewpoint and from all parts of the community, leading to new partnerships.

Reconciliation as action: Looking for understanding and forgiveness by acknowledging specific racial history and its effect on community life.

Personal responsibility: Recognizing that racism is everyone's problem and moving beyond pain and blame toward a constructive path of action.

Given the three goals listed above, think about the following questions:

1. In your community, what first steps might you take to begin to generate interest in these goals or to see if others would like to work toward using this national model?

____

____

____

____

2. If you find that there is interest, how might you make this a project that is "owned" by community members?

____

____

____

____

3. What steps might you and others take to move toward implementation?

____

____

____

____

4. How would you respond to criticism that this communication is important but that "all this talk doesn't really do anything but make people feel better"?

Community-Practice Exercise 10

Central Hill Community Center

Central Hill is an older neighborhood in a sprawling metropolitan area. The residents of Central Hill (approximately 4,000) are a diverse group in terms of ethnicity, race, and age. While other neighborhoods in the city have become more fragmented, there is a sense of cohesion within Central Hill. People tend to live there for many years. Residents look for ways to connect and show pride in their community, and they often hold street fairs and other outdoor events to demonstrate their sense of neighborhood. They call themselves a "vibrant" community, one in which there is a sense of hope for the future even though urban sprawl and an increasing crime rate in the larger metropolitan area comprise their larger environment.

Yet, Central Hill is a neighborhood where one in three residents is a child, in a community without a school, library, sit-down restaurant, post office, adult education, or job training center. With limited economic opportunities in this part of the city and no social center, residents feel pulled outside their local neighborhood for most services they need.

To focus fully on crime prevention, education, and revitalization efforts in Central Hill, a growing number of residents have been talking about developing a community center. Viewed as a "hub of activity" for residents and others interested in promoting a vital community, a center would be a safe place for learning and socializing. It would need to be located within walking distance of places of employment, maybe even offering a limited café menu so that people could chat over lunch or a cup of coffee. Perhaps it could be a place in which adult education and job-training programs are offered, bringing people together to learn new skills, thus benefitting individuals and the community as a whole.

You are a social work student who lives in the Central Hill community and you have been a part of the dialogue about a community center. Several people have mentioned the possibility of using the abandoned grocery store in the center of town. The owners moved to the strip mall on the periphery of the community last year because they needed more space. The store, now sitting idle, was once a hub for community shoppers, a place where one met neighbors as they pushed carts along the narrow aisles.

Preliminary conversations with the owners of the building have been encouraging. They, too, are members of the community and would be willing to sell the building at a reasonable price.

Yet, just purchasing the building will not be enough. Renovation will have to occur in order to transform the space into a useable, multipurpose community center. There are members of the community who are willing to donate time to renovation efforts, but they will need supplies and building materials to do the job.

Most Central Hill residents are excited about the ideas for the community center, but the plan is not without opposition. Some residents are worried that a community center would be "taken over" by persons outside the community who want to "hang out" and influence community youth in negative ways. Other residents are worried that it's too big a project to take on when there are other community needs to address. Still others are concerned that there will be initial enthusiasm but that the center will require sustained, ongoing oversight that will fall to a few people.

Consider the following questions in regard to Central Hill and its proposed community center:

1. The community center is seen as a solution. What are the needs in this community that would be addressed by a community center? Could other "solutions" or directions meet these needs? Does it have to be a community center? Why or why not?

____

____

____

____

____

2. If residents pursue the ideas for the community center, what steps would a professional social worker have to take in order to mobilize the community? Who would be the key stakeholders? Think particularly about those residents who are skeptical (for various reasons). How would you include them in this effort?

3. If residents pursue the community center, where would you, the social work student who lives in Central Hill, start? What are the things that have to be done? What additional questions or issues do these things raise?

4. If the community center is to be purchased, how would you begin a fund-raising drive to purchase the old grocery store? What would the drive be like? Where would donations come from? Would renting the building, at least initially, make sense?

5. If Central Hill residents were able to purchase the property, how would they obtain needed supplies and materials for renovation? How would you, as the social work student involved in the process, go about recruiting, overseeing, and supervising volunteer labor? How might you involve the full community in this effort?

Community-Practice Exercise 11

The Barrio Landlord

This exercise allows groups of students to proceed through a community intervention, step by step. After each section of the story, you will find a few short questions to answer before moving on to the next section. Fill in your answers on each page in the space provided. This way, as you contemplate the next section, you will have increased your knowledge and insight into the situation and will have advanced your intervention planning.

Week 1: The New Workers

Harry, Yolanda, Derrick, and Tamara are recent graduates of the University's M.S.W. program. They have taken advantage of an opportunity to work as members of an outreach team at Community House. Special grant funding has made this community-outreach project possible. Community House is a contemporary community center that traces it roots back eighty-five years to its beginnings as a settlement house. Its purpose is to provide social services to residents of the community located just outside the downtown area of an industrial city of 350,000. The center serves as a recreation and activity area for neighborhood youth after school and in the evening, operates a day-care program, provides educational and support groups for adults in the community, holds English classes for Spanish-speakers, and tries to provide other services as need arises. Before beginning to reach into the community, the new workers realize that they need to familiarize themselves fully with the agency.

1. What differences might there be between the present-day services provided and those that might have been provided when this agency was an actual settlement house?

2. In what agency documents might the workers look for information about the agency?

3. What resources might there be in the community that could help inform them about the agency? Are there other human service agencies and governmental units with information available? List the resources below.

Week 2: The Community Encounter

One day during their second week on the job, Harry and Yolanda take time at noon to walk around the neighborhood, familiarizing themselves with the environment. When they return, they inform Derrick and Tamara that there are some serious housing problems in the community that must contribute to human misery among the residents. They recall that they were told during their agency orientation meeting that affordable housing for working-class people can be difficult to obtain in this area and that what is available is often substandard.

They describe two apparently overcrowded apartment buildings near the center of the neighborhood. Two three-story buildings face each other across a small courtyard, with a six-foot latticework cement-block wall connecting the two buildings at the back of the lot. In front, there is a similar, but lower, wall separating a parking lot and the buildings from the busy street. Two dumpsters decorate the parking lot. Each apartment's front door is accessed via an open balcony on the front of the buildings. Functionally, the balconies serve as open corridors, with stairways located at each end of each building. On the rear of the buildings are small bedroom windows, and the front of the apartments have single picture windows facing the balconies. Overall, the buildings give the impression of once having served as a motel.

In addition to these observations, a chance conversation with a local storekeeper suggests that a number of the residents of the buildings are illegal aliens. The four new workers are very interested in this information because Community House traditionally serves any and all persons in the community, and works with people who need help obtaining citizenship. This might be a good place for them to start their outreach work.

1. There are many definitions of community. A generalized definition would emphasize the combination of social, economic, and governmental units that perform major functions for people. List some of these major functions and the units that perform them for the entire geographic community in which Community House is located.

2. In this scenario, there is a subcommunity within the larger community. How might you describe this subcommunity? What characterizes it in comparison to the larger community? In addition to economic and social factors, think about cultural factors. Write your description here.

3. Would this subcommunity have a collective identity? If so, describe the experiences, rituals, symbolic features, and values it might have.

Week 3: Seeing the Buildings

After discussing the conditions of this "barrio" among themselves, the new workers approach the agency director with their observations. The director indicates great familiarity with the apartments but says that no services are currently directed to this location and its residents. The director encourages them to seek out information about the characteristics of the residents living there, to do more analysis of the setting, and to check with the agency's experienced community organizers to see what additional information they can come up with before considering formulating a change effort.

The workers then decide to approach residents of the two apartment buildings. Derrick and Tamara undertake this because both have some elementary Spanish-language abilities. They find that there are many things wrong with the buildings. There is often no hot water, electrical wiring seems to be faulty, plumbing frequently backs up, and the courtyard and walkway are never cleaned. The dumpsters are overflowing and small. In short, the place is a mess. The four of them agree that they could not imagine living there.

1. What issues might Derrick and Tamara confront in approaching residents of the barrio?

2. Where in the community might the four community outreach workers locate information about the characteristics of the barrio's residents? List sources of information and then next to each item, indicate if it is an "official, formal source" or a "unofficial, informal source."

3. Does the information acquired to date suggest that there may be a target population for change efforts? Try to define it below.

4. List the social problems that appear to face the target population.

5. Are there possible elements of oppression faced by this population? If so, list them.

Week 4: The Barrio Landlord

When they discuss the concept of oppression and the target population, Yolanda asks, with some distaste in her voice, "I wonder who owns those buildings?" They realize they need to discover who owns the deplorable buildings. After all, someone should begin to advocate for residents' needs and see if basic repairs can be done. Tamara works quickly at the city tax office and finds that the owner is a prominent minister of a large suburban church.

After Harry, Yolanda, Derrick, and Tamara have acquired and analyzed this information, they approach the agency's most experienced community organizer who slowly shakes his head while telling them that the minister was approached by agency staff a couple of years ago. The minister had said that he was "doing God's will" and was providing housing for "God's unfortunates." The community organizer related that the discussion was polite and that it had been suggested to the minister, in a nonthreatening way, that it would be a good idea to make basic repairs because the building might otherwise be condemned by the city. The minister explained that he really didn't want to put any more money into the apartments because that would be a bad investment and that he would rather close them down, which he thought would be a terrible loss for the people living there, and for the community.

1. What is your reaction to this information? Are there any race or ethnic dimensions that should be considered?

2. What might you do now?

Community-Practice Activities

Community-Practice Activity A

Community Encounter

The following is an activity that may help you to begin to define a geographical context for community practice.

Step 1: Either walking or in a car, familiarize yourself with the geography of a community.
Step 2: Create a physical map of the area that notes the roadways; location and shape of neighborhood blocks; parks/open spaces; religious, educational, health, and/or social service resources; and commercial entities. Are there any special or unusual topographical features? See if you can draw in the community's boundaries.
Step 3: Look closely at the housing stock, other structures, sidewalks, and roadways and make judgments about the level of prosperity or decay of the "built environment."
Step 4: Identify the major physical strengths and weaknesses that should be considered prior to engaging in any neighborhood change action.

Community-Practice Activity B

Geographical Community Assessment

Using the following guide to understand the important dimensions of community functioning, complete a thorough assessment of the geography of a community.

Assessment Guide

I. General Information
  A. State, region, city
    1. Climate, type of soil (if important)
    2. Size, geographical boundaries, population
  B. History
    1. Date of founding of community, other important dates in the evolution of the community
    2. Time of year of most activity (for example, is this a summer community?)
    3. General status of community—growing, progressing, in what parts, what rhythm
  C. Population
    1. Who founded the community and how was it populated?
    2. Who are important families—historically? presently?
    3. What institutions or movements are focused on the development of the community? of social services?
  D. Who are the principal employers?
  E. Community organization
    1. Do conditions exist for group and institutional life?
    2. Is there development?

II. Family Life
  A. How many families live in the community?
  B. What is the average number of persons per home?
  C. What is the level of reported incidences of family violence?
  D. Are there activities that support family life?
  E. Are there activities for adolescents? Day care? Elder services?
  F. What might be done to improve family life?

III. Health
  A. Is there a hospital?
    1. Doctors?
    2. Dentists?
    3. Pharmacies?
    4. Other health services?
    5. Ambulance service?
  B. Are there problems with:
    1. Running water?
    2. Sewage disposal?
    3. Garbage disposal?
    4. Electricity?

C. How many ill people live in the community?
   1. What are the most frequent illnesses?
   2. Is AIDS a pressing problem?
   3. Other chronic/catastrophic illnesses?
D. What are some projects to protect or to better community health?

IV. Maintenance
   A. Is there a commercial district in the community or within easy reach?
      1. Grocery stores?
      2. Fast food?
      3. Bakeries?
      4. Clothing/department stores?
      5. Restaurants?
      6. Hotels?
   B. How many families lack basic necessities? What is the level of reliance on public assistance?
   C. What emergency and other social services are available?
   D. What are some projects that could improve how the community maintains itself?

V. Community Spirit
   A. Are there positive feelings between neighbors and families in the community?
      1. Accessible social clubs?
      2. Cooperatives?
      3. Associations?
   B. What is the level of hostility between families and groups in the community?
   C. What might be done to promote community spirit or unity?

VI. Recreation
   A. How many:
      1. Cinemas?
      2. Night clubs?
      3. Movie theaters?
      4. Bars?
      5. Sports fields?
      6. Bowling alleys?
      7. Basketball courts?
      8. Parks?
      9. Public open spaces?
   B. Is there community entertainment?
      1. Community music?
      2. Concerts?
      3. Community theaters?
      4. Organized sports?
   C. What TV program is most popular?
      1. Radio program?
   D. What do teenagers do in the evenings?
   E. What projects can be developed for more recreation or fun?

VII. Transportation
   A. Is there public transportation?
      1. Bus, train, plane service?
      2. Are taxis available?
   B. Do most people own cars?
      1. Commute to work?
      2. Carpool?

C. What are the road conditions?
   1. Are there tolls?
   2. Bridges?
   3. Are they governmentally or privately maintained?
   4. Are roads well maintained?

D. Are there traffic-pattern problems in the community?

E. What projects could be undertaken to facilitate secure, affordable, rapid transportation?

VIII. Communication

A. Do most people have phones in their homes or own cell phones?
   1. Are public phones available?
   2. How many TVs?
   3. Level of computer ownership?
   4. Newspapers?
   5. Post offices?
   6. Libraries?
   7. Newsstands?
   8. Radio stations?
   9. TV stations?
   10. Cable?

B. What is the literacy and language level of the community?

C. Does the community appear isolated? Connected regionally? Nationally? Internationally?

D. What projects might be executed to expand community connectivity?

IX. Education

A. What are the schools in the area?
   1. Levels?
   2. Public? Private?
   3. Perceived quality?

B. Is there a community college?
   1. Trade school?
   2. Literacy programs?
   3. GED programs?
   4. University?
   5. Other continuing education opportunities?

C. What is the school drop-out rate?

D. What programs can be developed to promote physical, artistic, professional, and intellectual development?

X. Economy

A. What is the median income?
   1. How many families seem to need financial aid?
   2. How many are considered well-to-do?

B. How many banks? Locally owned?
   1. Pawn shops?

C. What is the most common type of housing?
   1. How many rent?
   2. Is housing considered affordable?
   3. How many are homeless?
   4. How many people own their own dwelling?

D. What is the rate of employment?
   1. Are employees in the service or manufacturing industry?
   2. Other?

E. What projects might be undertaken for economic recuperation for the community?
   1. For the less fortunate?
   2. How can financial resources be developed in the area?

XI. Production
   A. Is there farm production in the area?
      1. Ranches?
      2. Poultry farms?
      3. Cattle? Pork production?
      4. What type of agriculture is in the area?
      5. Are these large or small properties?
      6. What is the proportion of family farms to agribusinesses?
      7. Where does the farm production go?
   B. Is there forest production in the area?
   C. Is there industry?
      1. Factories?
      2. Arts and craft production?
      3. Mining?
      4. Small business?
   D. Are unions important in the community?
   E. What projects could be undertaken to augment production, jobs, or better labor conditions.

XII. Religion/Spirituality
   A. How many churches, synagogues, and mosques are in the community?
      1. What religious organizations are active in the area?
      2. What would be considered the level of religiosity in the area?
      3. Is it considered conservative or liberal?
   B. How many people do not have a religious preference?
   C. Does Satanism or the occult have influence in the area?
   D. What about New-Age religions? Yoga? Shamanism?
   E. What projects might be undertaken for spiritual development?

XIII. Safety
   A. What is the judicial district? (Judicial districts tell us something of what type of judge is involved.)
   B. Are there police stations? Sheriff's department?
   C. How many law enforcement officers are in the community? State police?
   D. Are there military installations?
      1. National guard?
      2. Military reserve units?
   E. Are there private detectives?
   F. Are there private security guards?
   G. Are there fire stations or public-safety stations?
      1. How many firefighters?
      2. Emergency medical technicians?
      3. Paid or volunteer?
   E. Are there dangerous locations in the community?
      1. Dangerous groups?
      2. Gangs?
      3. Drug trade?
      4. Violence?
      5. Other activities that take away from family tranquility?
   F. Are there projects that could promote peace and order in the community?

XIV. Politics/Public Service

A. Is the community a part of a government entity?
   1. Describe the governing structure.
   2. Who represents the community in local, state, and national politics?

B. What public services are available in the community?

C. What is the general level of political involvement in the area?

D. What are the current unmet community requests of local government?

E. How many are registered to vote? What is the level of voter participation?

F. What are possible projects to take advantage of or complement public services?

XV. Justice

A. Are there institutions of justice in the area?
   1. Family courts?
   2. Criminal courts?
   3. Law offices?
   4. Legal aid?

B. Do community members participate regularly on juries?

C. Are there apparent problems with civil rights?
   1. Illegal activities?

D. What can be done to promote the rights and civic duties of community residents?

XVI. Community Pride

A. Are there community heroes?
   1. Monuments?
   2. Commemorative plaques?

B. Is there knowledge of community history?
   1. What are the most important facts about this community?
   2. Who are the principal personalities?

C. Are there points of interest?
   1. Picturesque areas?
   2. Places of interest to tourists?

D. Are the residents welcoming? Indifferent? Hostile?

E. Who is considered the primary benefactor of the community?

F. What projects could augment the merit, prestige, pride of the community?

XVII. Miscellaneous

A. What norms and values predominate in the community?

B. How would you characterize the general community feeling?

C. What is the general community personality?

D. What seem to be community goals?

E. What are the strengths of the community?

F. What challenges does this community face?

Summary Assessment

1. Based on your assessment of the community, what are the two changes you see that could improve community life?

___

___

___

2. What systems are in place that could be used in any change action?

___

___

___

3. What people might be available to aid in the change action?

___

___

___

4. What would be your first step, if you were to design a community change action?

___

___

___

5. Would community development, social action, or social planning be required?

___

___

___

Community-Practice Activity C

The Barrio Landlord

Refer back to the scenario of this name in the Community Exercise section of this book.

This individual, outside-of-class activity, provides an opportunity to apply concepts concerning community, community assessment, target populations, and community human-services systems. After reading the Barrio Landlord (see pages 137–141) scenario and related exercises concerning community and human-service systems, answer the following items.

The Problem and the Target Population

1. Describe what you consider to be the social condition in this situation.

2. Who is the target population? How would you define the target population?

3. How could you assess the needs of the target population?

4. Where would you go in the larger community for data about available social services?

5. What is the problem in this situation? Write a problem definition.

Community

1. Define the "barrio" community.

2. From reading the case, what other communities could you project as existing in the urban environment around the barrio community?

3. Using a broad definition of community, think of, and list, any communities (of place, group with a common interest, or identity) that may exist in this environment that may be relevant in intervention planning.

Human-Service Delivery Systems

1. What formal agency and program service delivery units might one expect to be available to residents of the barrio? You might wish to list these by category: public (governmental), not-for-profit, and for profit.

   - Public:

   - Not-for-profit:

   - For profit:

2. List informal service-providing units that might exist for residents of the barrio.

3. List intermediary or mediating units that may exist.

4. What potential strengths in the human-service delivery system could be called upon in making changes in this community?

5. List barriers that will likely be present that can prevent formal and mediating services from reaching members of the barrio community.

Part 4

Organization Practice

Keywords:

agency, assessment, budgeting, decision making, evaluability, goals, metaphors, needs assessment, objectives, outcomes, organization, organization practice, program, service, strategic planning, supervision

Introduction

This section on organization practice focuses on the ever-changing nature of life in organizations. Like communities, organizations are arenas in which policy is often implemented. Therefore, you will recognize here themes covered in earlier sections, themes that are continued and expanded as building blocks of contextual decision making in organizations. The chart that follows categorizes materials according to those that demystify organizations, help in conceptualizing and defining organizations, increase organizational sensitivity, facilitate practicing organization-related tasks, and enhance organization-change skills. Through exercises and activities we will illustrate the importance of understanding organizational structure and developing sensitivities to behavior within organizations; then move to planning for organizational change, implementing change, and the importance of continual organizational development.

We believe well-developed organizational skills are necessary for *all* professional social workers, regardless of micro or macro practice interests. All social workers will be expected to perform professionally in the context of some sort of organization. It is the rare social worker who is able to perform as a totally independent agent, and even if he or she can, interaction with organizations on behalf of clients will be an ongoing concern. Given this almost universal need to be a competent member of some sort of organization, this section of the workbook contains exercises and activities that focus on assessing and diagnosing organizations; planning and implementing change in the organizational structure or in service programming; and evaluating change.

It is essential to develop well-honed organizational assessment and diagnostic skills, just as it is to develop direct-practice assessment and diagnostic skills. In order to accomplish this, opportunities to understand the characteristics of organizations and their approaches to practice will be provided. Critical thinking and ethical judgment will also come into play because our expectation is that the values of the social work profession, which are the foundational base of our profession, will take precedence in your assessment and diagnostic work. When you finish your work in this section, we want you to know what it means to exercise social work skills and values in the organizations where you are called to practice as a social worker.

Once the assessment skills are in place, decision-making, planning, and teamwork skills become important tools for success in any organizational or programmatic change action. We will provide various opportunities to extend your decision-making, planning, and communication skills. Some of these skills will be transferred from what you have learned in the policy and community-practice sections. Setting priorities, managing boundaries and emotions within an organizational context, as well as overall organizational survival skills will be tested here in order to enable you to think critically and flourish individually and professionally in ever-changing, stressful, fast-paced organizational settings.

"The Days of Our Placements: Scene V"

With the blessings and encouragement of the others, Maria had proceeded to organize community meetings of parents with elementary-age children to explore the issues involved in after-school care and identify the needs expressed by the parents themselves. Meanwhile, the Community House administration asked Yusof and Tamara to go to a "street meeting" for people living on Nice Street that had been called by a retired social worker who lived on the street. Mr. Williams (he was always addressed as Mr.) was respected in the community for the work he had done in establishing a very successful community-action program in the 1960s. Mr. Williams had asked Community House to send an agency official in the hopes that the agency might help. Tamara and Yusof reported after the meeting that Mr. Williams, with whom they were quite impressed, wanted to mobilize the street to resist an invasion of city workers and equipment that were tearing up the street, supposedly to improve the flow of traffic. They reported that the plan was to make the street one-way to speed the flow of traffic, and residents were alarmed because they had preferred that traffic be slowed to preserve the calm of their neighborhood and to make it safer for children and older people crossing Nice Street. Further, the construction was leaving mud all over and dangerous open holes.

Meeting with all five of the students to review progress in various areas, the field instructor recommended asking if the Executive Director would formally commit agency resources to cosponsoring the Nice Street effort. Tamara and Yusof did this and reported back the following week that while concerned for the residents, the Executive Director has indicated that he would have to check with "his" board and with certain elected city officials about this. He had mentioned in concluding the meeting with the two students that he was not sure the agency mission included work with the city in this manner. Tamara said that sounded confusing but that she did not feel she could question the Executive Director about the statement. After some discussion as to why the Executive Director might appear to be cautious, Harry said, in his usual style, "If the E.D. thinks the mission statement is important in this, then shouldn't we get on top of that and take a look at it? After all, missions can change, can't they?" Chrystal, somewhat hesitantly, added what turned out to be a minor bombshell, saying that her father, who did independent consulting, audit, and accounting work for government units in the area, had told her that he had noticed that Community House seemed to be doing pretty well since it appeared to have more contracts with the city for service provision than did any other local social service agency. Yusof jumped in instantly, saying now he thought he saw why one resident at the meeting had referred to community house as "an establishment agency."

At this point, the field instructor reminded them of the importance of critical thinking, suggesting that an analysis of the agency position in the community, its funding sources, and its commitment to area residents would be appropriate before jumping to conclusions. In conclusion, the field instructor said that at their next meeting, they should look not only at the mission statement of the agency but its stated goals and outcome evaluation studies and try to link all that to the change actions they were planning.

Organization Practice: Exercise and Activity Chart		
Focus	**Exercises**	**Activities**
Demystifying Organizations	Exercise 1: Organizational Metaphors	Activity A: Know Your Agency
Conceptualizing and Defining Organizations	Exercise 2: Organization-Practice Definitions	Activity B: Organizational Categories
Increasing Organizational Sensitivity	Exercise 3: What-If Scenarios Exercise 4: Job Descriptions Exercise 5: Ethical Supervision	Activity C: Organizational Cultural Competence
Practicing Organization-Related Tasks	Exercise 6: Supportive Supervision Exercise 7: Billable Hours Exercise 8: The Electronic Highway Exercise 9: Needs Assessment Data Exercise 10: Fairview Family Services Exercise 11: The "Age Power" Budget	Activity D: Program Assessment Activity E: Funding One's Program Activity F: Political–Economic Context Activity G: Evergreen Agency Memo Activity H: Strategic-Planning Analysis
Enhancing Organization-Change Skills	Exercise 12: Budgetary Shortfall Exercise 13: Agency Reorganization Exercise 14: Neighborhood House	Activity I: Evaluability Assessment Activity J: Sunnyview In Basket

Organization-Practice Exercises

Organization-Practice Exercise 1

Organizational Metaphors

In *Images of Organizations* (1997)[1] Gareth Morgan attempted to demystify one's ability to understand and transform organizations and situations in them by identifying images or metaphors used to see, understand, and manage organizations. Metaphors serve as a link to organizational theory and can be useful in learning about how one practices in organizational settings.

Step 1: In the chart that follows, provide an example of an organization you are familiar with that might reflect each image or metaphor.
Step 2: What are the advantages/disadvantages of using each metaphor? Jot notes in the chart below.
Step 3: Now, choose your own metaphor to describe the nature of human-service organizations. What are the advantages and limitations of the metaphor?

Metaphor/Image Chart			
Image or Metaphor	**An Example from Your Experience**	**Strengths**	**Weaknesses**
Organization as a machine			
Organization as an organism			
Organization as a brain			
Organization as a culture			
Organization as a psychic prison			
Organization as flux and transformation			
Organization as domination			
Your metaphor: ______________________			

[1]Morgan, G. (1997). *Images of Organizations* (2nd ed.). Thousand Oaks, CA: Sage.

Organization-Practice Exercise 2

Organization-Practice Definitions

To increase understanding of organizations and their functioning, in a work group discuss each of the following terms. Write as complete a definition as possible without regard to the size or type of organization to which the terms might apply:

1. Bureaucracy

2. Organizational authority

3. Organizational structure

4. Organizational behavior

5. Organizational culture

6. Task environment

7. Association

8. Ideological community

____

____

____

9. Franchise

____

____

____

10. Host organization

____

____

____

On returning to the larger classroom setting, compare and contrast the definitions from each group and discuss implications of the differences for organization practice.

Organization-Practice Exercise 3

What-If Scenarios

Policies may mandate programs that address social problems, but communities and organizations give life to program implementation. Consider the following scenarios in light of the policy/program connection in organizations.

Scenario One

Current law and regulations require unwed mothers receiving public assistance to cooperate with the department of social services in naming and locating the father of their child.

- How might you implement this policy if you were a caseworker who strongly believed in this policy?

___

___

___

- How might you implement this policy if you were strongly opposed to it?

___

___

___

Scenario Two

You work for a small nonprofit social service agency that has just been mandated to have at least one bilingual social worker on the staff if it is to continue to receive funding for one of its major programs. Currently the agency has no one on staff who is bilingual and no vacant positions.

- What implementation issues might this raise for the agency and the management?

___

___

___

___

- What are the staff issues involved here?

___

___

___

___

___

Scenario Three

You are a medical social worker who has been asked to be the organ transplant designee for the hospital employing you. This, according to policy, means that you are required to approach any patient who is dying to determine their willingness to be an organ donor.

- What implementation issues does this raise?

____

____

____

- How might the policy be monitored and evaluated?

____

____

____

- What patient information would be appropriate for these purposes?

____

____

____

Scenario Four

The Older Americans Act requires each state receiving funding under the Act to have a designated long-term-care ombudsperson. The ombudsperson is responsible for responding to complaints relating to conditions in facilities that care for elders (such as nursing homes, adult-care homes, rehabilitation facilities). Each state is also required to have a comprehensive reporting system for complaints received through the ombudsperson program.

- What monitoring issues would need to be considered in meeting these mandates?

____

____

____

- How might the effectiveness of the ombudsperson program be evaluated?

____

____

____

- What evaluation criteria might be employed?

____

____

____

Organization-Practice Exercise 4

Job Descriptions

Read the following letter. Then, as a group, discuss the questions that follow the letter.

HUEY, DEWY, CHEATEM & HOW
COUNSELORS AT LAW
. . . moving the world

March 24, 2004

Richard Lafayette, Services Supervisor
Excellent Agency
1006 East Boulevard
Anytown, USA 33340

Dear Richard:

I thought it would be a good idea to take a few minutes out from my work here at the firm to inform you of a situation that would appear to want attention at the agency.

Three staff members from the agency have contacted me in the last few days. They thought that since I am President of the Board of Directors that I might be able to help straighten out a concern they had. All three indicate that they were assigned responsibilities not related to what they were hired to do. They are concerned that they are not trained to do this work and that clients may not receive the level of service they deserve. Also, they feel that they should not be evaluated on tasks for which they are not trained.

You and I know one another well, and I'm sure this can be worked out. I wonder if the staff job descriptions reflect these new duties? Will they be evaluated on activities for which they are not trained? Further, these concerns may reflect a larger problem within the agency—that of staff morale. It seems that we need to look at this situation seriously. I thought I would direct this matter to you since you are responsible for the agency's service delivery staff.

With our continuing efforts to improve the agency, it would seem that this matter should be quickly addressed. Could you give me a call as soon as you can? Many thanks.

Sincerely,

Meredith Light
President
Board of Directors

1. What issues in this letter relate to the relationship of agency administration, agency staff, and the board of directors of private, not-for-profit, or for-profit agencies?

2. What principles related to agency management may be relevant here?

Organization-Practice Exercise 5

Ethical Supervision

For each of the following situations, indicate if an ethical issue or behavior in supervision is reflected in the description. As a group, discuss why or why not.

1. In a not-for-profit agency, in an effort to gain approval from the board to create a new position for a bilingual social worker, a supervisor purposely exaggerates the number of Hispanic clients the unit is serving.
2. A supervisor, who personally disagrees with a recently enacted agency policy, encourages employees who are adversely affected by the policy to pressure higher level agency administrators to change the policy.
3. A supervisor, employed by a private, not-for-profit Catholic agency that has taken a firm stand against abortion, encourages supervisees to provide information to their pregnant clients as to where they might obtain information about abortion.
4. A supervisor for a private, not-for-profit, in-home health service that subsidizes services to isolated, poor, elderly individuals reviews a referral form from another agency along with an application for subsidized in-home health services. The supervisor recognizes the name of the potential new client and realizes that the age stated on both forms is five years below the agency's eligibility standard for subsidized services. The supervisor approves subsidized services for the new client.
5. A female supervisor belongs to a social organization that does not admit men to membership.
6. Knowing there is a long waiting list, a supervisor in an adult day-care program asks the program's director to immediately admit the supervisor's mother to the program.

Organization-Practice Exercise 6

Supportive Supervision

You are the supervisor of a unit of social workers whose jobs call for the provision of counseling and other services to birth parents whose child is in foster care, with the goal of family reunification. Workers are expected to meet with parents twice per month, arrange weekly parent/child visitations, develop case plans that focus on overcoming deficits, and be available to respond to birth-parent questions and concerns.

Through your regular review of logs, case-progress notes, case plans, and your personal observations, as well as behavior in unit meetings, you suspect that there is some sort of a problem bothering one of your workers. Performance seems to be declining and the worker is not as prompt as in the past. You suspect burnout due to the stresses of the job and a lack of job satisfaction. Plan a supervisory conference in which you will support this staff person while not overlooking the quality of service delivery and goal accomplishment sought in the unit. Below, create an agenda for this conference, outlining the steps and content for the conference.

The agenda will include:

Steps I might take:

Content to be covered:

Organization-Practice Exercise 7

Billable Hours

You are the head of a department at a large social service organization. You have the following assignment from the service's division director to whom you report:

> Please institute a change in client–worker contact hours. More billable hours will be required in the future. This may mean fewer pro bono hours and less stretching of the standard 50-minute "contact hour" by unit staff. We need to make this shift by the beginning of the next quarter.

You recognize immediately that this may change the type of client who will be receiving services. You also know the perspective of your service-unit workers who favor accessible, affordable services for those most in need.

Below, compose a memorandum to persuade the service-unit workers to comply with agency mandates.

If you had not been directed to write the memo, what else might you have done to increase either billable hours or overall agency income?

Organization-Practice Exercise 8

The Electronic Highway

Instructions

The following exercise describes a day in the life of a services supervisor. It can be used as a role-play situation or as a group discussion of what this person would do.

The Setting and Your Position

You are the services supervisor for an urban community center serving homeless people, many of whom suffer from mental disabilities of one sort or another. They also tend to have unresolved health problems and difficulty obtaining and holding decent jobs. On the whole, the consumers of the agency's services appreciate what the agency does.

You are completing your third year in the agency and in this job, and you like your work. Your position is important in assuring that clients are served in an appropriate and timely manner. You are one of two staff members reporting to the agency executive director. The other administrative staff person is the assistant director for fiscal affairs. An administrative assistant provides support to the director, the assistant director, and you. You are responsible for supervising five program coordinators who head the five service units that are organized according to their service purpose and function. These units are:

- Intake and dayroom activities
- In-house employment, day-labor placement, job development and training
- Temporary, overnight quarters
- Substance-abuse treatment
- Health screening and health education

The Situation

Arriving at work at 8:00 a.m. on Monday, you find that the agency computer system was put out of commission by a power surge resulting from an early-morning lightning strike. As the administrative assistant tells you this, you recall the storm waking you up early that morning. You quickly realize there is no back-up system to provide access to computerized data and records. The computer system is composed of personal computers located in the administrative offices and the offices of each service unit, and they are networked together. In addition, several portable computers are shared among staff at times when they have to be in the field; staff download data to the network on returning to the office.

The administrative assistant tells you that the five unit supervisors are now in the room known affectionately as the "bull pen," a large, general-purpose room that serves as meeting and work space. They are discussing, in a somewhat hurried manner, how their units are going to be able to function that day. None of them has enough knowledge about the network to be able to evaluate what is wrong, but it is clear to them that the network and the individual machines are not functioning. A call has gone out to the computer company that installed and services the network. The company promises to have a service person there by noon. They also assure you they can have the system up and running by 3:00 p.m. If not, they will bring in loaner equipment to make it work by 8:00 a.m. the following day.

Confronting the Situation

Entering the bull pen, you realize that the supervisors are close to panicking as they wonder what to do next. You also know that the agency executive director is on the way to the Amtrak station to catch a 9:00 a.m. train for Washington for a federal-grant-funding meeting. You sit down with the supervisors to sort things out and to help them get things going for the day. Discussion that follows determines that each of the units is dependent on the networked computer system for different things, and the notes you make during the discussion reflect this, as follows:

- *Intake and dayroom activities*—recording information on new members (clients) who may show up any time of day, usually beginning at about 9:00 a.m.
- *Employment*—two things: 1) the daily work rotation assignment schedule for members who work internally within the agency, and 2) the daily work schedule for members who hire out to small businesses and contractors as day labor.
- *Temporary, overnight quarters*—a list of those persons who qualify to stay overnight and a list of those who have used up their limit of nights are kept on computer.
- *Substance abuse*—client treatment plans, including daily medication schedules, are stored on computer.
- *Health*—the health records of members under medical supervision are computerized. The visiting physician and nurse are due at 10:00 a.m. to administer psychotropic medications. They use the records for patient dosage and frequency, updating them daily.

What to Do?

By the time you have gathered this information, it is 9:15 a.m. You are scheduled to conduct a final employment interview at 9:30 a.m. with an outside candidate who is a potential new supervisor (one of your staff is leaving in a week and must be replaced). At 11:00 a.m. you are due at a United Way Allocations Hearing to defend the budget of the agency's health screening and health-education program; you are to stand in for the director in this activity. You are also the designated "Officer of the Day" for the agency while the executive director is away.

"Yikes," you think to yourself, "what do I do next?" You decide to organize your thoughts in the form of an organized, ordered list of how you will proceed through the rest of the day. Your assumption is that a little time invested now will pay off later in the day.

What would be on your list?

Organization-Practice Exercise 9

Needs Assessment Data

You are a group of staff in a regional planning agency that covers 15 counties, one eighth of the counties in the state in which you are located. A comprehensive needs assessment has never been conducted in your region to determine the needs of persons who provide care for various population groups (such as, elders, disabled people, young children). If you wanted to collect usable data that would help in your planning, what would you do? Begin by responding to the questions below:

1. Who do you think would also want to have these data collected?

2. Who might use these data once they are collected, and for what purposes?

3. How would having new information about caregivers contribute to their well-being?

4. Do you think it would be more helpful to conduct a consumer/client needs assessment, a provider needs assessment, or both? Why or why not?

5. Who would likely collect these data?

6. Would a sample be developed? If yes, why would you consider using a sample? If so, how would you develop it?

7. Would you use quantitative or qualitative methods, or both?

8. What methods of data collection might you use?

9. Could you use existing data to help in your design?

10. What are the strengths and weaknesses of the data collection methods you would use?

11. What are the logical steps you would take to implement the design?

12. What questions are likely to remain unanswered by your plan?

13. How would you use these data in your planning efforts?

Organization-Practice Exercise 10

Fairview Family Services

Fairview Family Services is a well-established family-services agency located in a large metropolitan area in the mid-Atlantic region. It is one of the oldest nonprofit agencies in the area, with a long history of a variety of services for families in need. Originally established in 1910 as a safe haven for mothers and children, its service picture has changed over the years as community needs have changed.

Because of its longevity, Fairview has a small endowment that is currently used to maintain its main offices located in a building built for the agency in 1915 (approximately 5 percent of budget). Other sources of funding include the United Way (20 percent of budget); fees for services (15 percent of budget); state family-violence funds (24 percent of budget); and two annual fund-raisers and ongoing solicitation, which must provide the remaining 36 percent of budget. For the last two years there has been a slight shortfall (less than 2 percent each year) that has required dipping into the principal of the endowment.

The board has become increasingly concerned about the financial stability of the agency, particularly its reliance on grant funding. The finance committee was recently expanded to include fund-raising, as well as financial stewardship. Four new businesspeople have been added to the committee to increase board fund-raising capacity. Currently, there is discussion about the potential of changing the agency mission to focus more directly on clients who can pay for services. The idea is to expand day care and clinical service so that fees for service represent at least one quarter of the budget.

The agency director is a social worker trained in planning and administration with about twenty years of experience in social work practice. She came to the agency about five years ago because she was excited about the agency's history of serving the underserved, especially women and children. She was also drawn to its violence prevention and trauma remediation programs. She thought that she had the skill and expertise to move the agency into the position of community leader regarding family violence prevention. This is her commitment to the agency and its employees.

Most of the agency employees are not professionally trained, but have come up through the ranks of volunteer and paraprofessional service. Though several have advanced degrees in social work and counseling, little notice is given to professional training. Instead, experience with the agency is what counts. A split is developing between professionally educated workers and those with life and work experience. Those with clinical training are looking forward to a more orderly service-delivery experience providing either early-childhood education or clinical programs to willing clients who can pay their way. The older, paraprofessional employees see this shift as a disastrous move away from the clients most in need of services. They see the board as responsible for finding funds to support current programs, instead of placing the responsibility for service access with clients.

Adding to the pressure is the need to implement what was proposed in the five-year grant for community violence prevention, plus some indications from United Way that, of programs to which United Way provides funds, the client profiles do not proportionally represent the racial and ethnic makeup of its catchment area. In other words, not enough minority families are being served by these programs.

In order to remedy both of these challenges, the director has entered into a process of collaborative planning with Child League, a traditionally African-American, child-serving agency in the inner city. This agency is even older than Fairview Family Services, having been established by a church group around the time of the Civil War. It has a continuous history of community outreach, early-childhood education and family support. It is one stable element in a very challenging community environment fraught with the consequences of poverty, isolation, and lack of service access.

The executive director of Child League is also a trained social worker with more than 25 years experience with this agency and the community it serves. He has entered into a collaborative planning process with the director of Fairview because he sees the need for more clinical services that his staff cannot provide. He also sees the possibility of leveraging this collaboration into more resources for his agency and the community. He understands that this collaboration means no real money for his agency, but he sees the possibilities of in-kind services and is willing to move forward if he can be sure that the service-delivery package in this community is controlled by Child League.

The workers at Child League are community leaders who have moved into the organization from their lives in this community. With the exception of the program director, a social worker, and the day-care director, no one has advanced degrees. Only about one quarter of the staff have undergraduate degrees or some college. They have heard about the collaborative venture and are suspicious of the activity. This is not the first time that outside agencies and people have thought that they could do a better job than they currently do to overcome the very real consequences of social problems this community faces on a daily basis. To a person, they would rather develop a new clinical program than open their door to outsiders.

Based on negotiations between the two directors, and with the approval of both boards, the two Fairview social workers funded by grant monies will be outplaced at Child League. Their responsibilities will be direct clinical services to families dealing with family violence and teaming with Child League workers to develop community-wide violence-prevention activities. Any funds raised for community activities will go to Child League through a subcontract for services.

The two Fairview social workers slotted for this work have been with the agency for three and five years, respectively. Both are female Caucasians with little cross-cultural experience. They realize that they must accept this new assignment or potentially lose their jobs. Their friends and colleagues at Fairview feel their ambivalence, but no one is talking about this new challenge for fear of being perceived as racist. Most other employees are just glad they have not been given this new assignment.

The employees at Child League don't know what to think after the first meeting with the Fairview workers—who seemed afraid and uncertain. It left a bad taste all around. The program directors from both agencies have been told by their executive directors to see that this effort succeeds.

As a group, discuss the following questions:

1. What are your assumptions about this situation? From a micro or direct-practice perspective? From a macro or administrative perspective?

____

____

____

____

2. What are the problems and issues in this situation?

____

____

____

____

3. From a professional administrative and planning perspective, what do you think is needed? For Fairview? For Child League?

____

____

____

____

4. From a professional clinical perspective what is needed? For Fairview? For Child League?

____

____

____

____

5. What would you do if you were a social worker called in to consult about future directions for these agencies?

Organization-Practice Exercise 11

The "Age Power" Budget

You are a group of experts from the community that has been called together by the executive director of the Area Agency on Aging. Some special initiative funds have been allocated by the state to do one-time projects that will enhance the physical and emotional needs of seniors. Your job is to look over the proposed budgets of the various agencies that have responded to the RFP (request for proposals) and to ask relevant questions about what they propose to do.

The proposal you currently have before you is called "Age Power" and is designed to enhance seniors' lives through physical fitness. Carefully study the budget that follows and the justification they have proposed and decide what questions you want to ask their representatives about the budget and its justification when they appear before you to defend their proposal. List your questions below:

____

____

____

____

____

____

Sample Budget—FY 2003–04—"Age Power" Program

Line Item	Funding Requested	Cash (In-Kind)	Totals
Salaries and Wages			
1. Program Director (¼ time)	$ 15,000		$ 15,000
2. Program Manager (FT)	$ 45,000		$ 45,000
3. Volunteer Coordinator (½ time)	$ 20,000		$ 20,000
4. Counselor (FT)	$ 40,000		$ 40,000
Employee-Related Expenses (@27%)	$ 32,400		$ 32,400
Total Personnel Costs	**$152,400**		**$152,400**
Other Operating Expenses			
5. Curriculum Development	$ 2,000		$ 2,000
6. Fitness Supplies	$ 1,000	$1,000	$ 2,000
7. Office Supplies	$ 2,400		$ 2,400
8. Client Transportation		$6,000	$ 6,000
9. Telephone	$ 1,200		$ 1,200
Total Other Operating Expenses	**$ 6,600**	**$7,000**	**$ 13,600**
Total Personnel and Other Operating Expenses	**$159,000**	**$7,000**	**$166,000**
Indirect Costs @ 10% allowable by funding source	$ 15,900		$ 15,900
Total Program Costs	**$174,900**	**$7,000**	**$181,900**

Budget Justification for "Age Power" Program	
1. Program Director (¼ time)	Program director is also overseeing Elder Rights and Senior Power programs. \$60,000 × ¼ time = \$15,000. Director will supervise other staff and provide program oversight.
2. Program Manager (FT)	Full-time M.S.W. credentialed program manager @ \$45,000. (See attached job description.)
3. Volunteer Coordinator (½ time)	Volunteer coordinator is half time with Elder Rights program. \$40,000 × ½ = \$20,000. (See attached job description.)
4. Counselor (FT)	To be hired @ \$40,000 per year. (See attached job description.)
5. Curriculum Development	Covers books and registration fees for 35 older adults participating in fitness program.
6. Fitness Supplies	Covers yoga mats, step equipment, and weights. Note the \$1,000 requested is being matched by Fitness International's contribution of weights.
7. Office Supplies	\$200 per month to cover paper, toner cartridges, pens/pencils, envelopes, and stationery.
8. Client Transportation	Donated in-kind by volunteers who provide transportation to and from fitness events.
9. Telephone	\$100 per month to cover installation and long-distance costs.

Organization-Practice Exercise 12

Budgetary Shortfall: A Role Play

Directions

This in-class exercise provides an opportunity for students to role-play various positions within a county welfare department that is facing a budgetary shortfall. The scripts are designed to illustrate various perspectives one might find in an organization that is struggling with cutback management. Six students will need to volunteer for this role play. The rest of the class can observe and take notes that can be used in debriefing what occurs.

The Context

The agency context in which this role play occurs is the county welfare department. The county has mandated that the welfare office cut the budget for the social services division by 25%, about $125,000. All the major administrators are now meeting to decide how to manage the mandate. The agenda for today's meeting is to develop the plan for reducing expenditures. Those present are the director, the assistant director, the fiscal officer, the director of income maintenance, the director of social services, and because Child Protective Services (CPS) represents the lion's share of the service budget, the CPS supervisor.

The Role of the Director

You are the director of the county welfare department. You have never been in awe of bureaucracies, and you are obviously interested in changing the culture of the department if you can possibly make any inroads while you are here. You've read all the books you could find on organizational culture and leadership and you sincerely believe that leadership can effect change. Since you have limited patience and high energy, you often act quickly and sometimes intentionally outrageously to put people off guard and to demonstrate alternative ways of viewing organizations. You are hoping to change this organization's culture, and you talk about that all the time.

As you play your role, you will focus on changing norms and demonstrating new behavioral artifacts (interactions) that may not be typical in this organization. Your task in this role play is to bring out the theoretical perspectives of organizational culture so that the observers will see how theoretical concepts can be applied. For example, you use words like norms, culture, artifacts, assumptions, and cultural roots as you meet with your colleagues. You will focus on how implementation of this budgetary change will affect the culture in which this agency operates, and you are dead set against people who reflect traditional orientations.

The Role of the Assistant Director

You are the assistant director in the county welfare department and you are not a friend of the director. You believe in bureaucracy and your motto is that there should be a clear division of labor, established roles, and hierarchical organizational charts in all agencies. You are sick and tired of cries for diversity that only take people away from what they are supposed to do. You believe that bureaucracy is the best way to control situations, and you have always used your legal/rational authority to keep people in their place in this agency. You continue to want to do so, and when it comes to implementing any plans in this agency you want to be sure the rules are clearly spelled out so that everyone knows exactly what they must do.

In this role play you are constantly stressing the importance of key bureaucratic concepts such as hierarchy, division of labor, clear rules, control, compliance, and authority. You want this change to be implemented in an efficient manner and you are more concerned about maintaining the structure of the agency than you are about the people within the organization. You are the ultimate bureaucrat, and you absolutely hate the director, who is always talking about how to change the organization's culture.

The Role of the Financial Officer

You are the financial officer of the county welfare department. You have been educated to believe strongly in scientific management theory. In fact, life would be reasonably simple if staff in this agency would just understand that things have to be done in as efficient a manner as possible. You are a proponent of a "mean, lean, organization" and you are a proud owner of an M.B.A. degree. You get somewhat frustrated with social workers who seem to dwell on process so much of the time. Implementation to you means that the process is only a well-oiled means to an appropriate product. You are looking for the most efficient manner in which implementation can occur.

In this role play, you want others to embrace your theoretical perspective. This means that you will be talking about scientific management principles such as the importance of efficiency, the need for caseload and workload studies to see how implementation is working, and the importance of flowcharting to demonstrate the "one best way" to do things. You get very frustrated that others can't see the logic in there being "one best way" and you are constantly reminding them of this principle.

The Role of the Director of Income Maintenance

You are the director of income maintenance in the county welfare department. You have been in this position for a long time and you believe strongly in systems theory. In implementing any decision, you know that inputs, throughputs, outputs, and outcomes must all be considered so that there are indicators at each stage of implementation as to how things are going. You are very concerned about process and worry that people lose sight of the importance of intervention options in their race for a final product. You believe implementation has to be systematic and thoughtful, and there must be a well-designed information system to capture what happens. This takes time and attention to detail.

You constantly use systems language in this role play, talking about the importance of organizational boundaries, organizational maintenance, the relationship of the organization to its environment, the turbulence in the environment, contingencies that have to be considered, and the uncertainty faced by the agency in implementing what needs to be done. When other people think in a closed-systems manner, you are quick to point out that implementation cannot occur in a vacuum.

The Role of the Director of Social Services

As director of social services for the county welfare department, you are a believer in human relations theory. You are an M.S.W. and it has been drilled into you that group dynamics, human behavior, and a host of other factors are the important elements of the work that you and your staff do. You are getting frustrated with the cry for outcome measurement, which seems to be done "at all costs," and you want the participation of staff and consumers to be heard in the implementation process. You feel, at times, like you are crying in the wilderness, but you are constantly asking how people will think and feel about what they do in their work.

You use concepts like informal group and the importance of motivating people. You see implementation occurring only if the leaders of this agency (including yourself) recognize the importance of human dynamics and group interaction in getting things done. You have been known to mumble under your breath that Elton Mayo would be rolling over in his grave when people do not recognize the importance of human relations in your organization.

The Role of the CPS Supervisor

You are the CPS supervisor of the county welfare department. You feel like you have seen it all, for you have been in public welfare services for a number of years. You are an M.S.W. and you are proud to be part of a profession that views social justice as a guiding principle in their code of ethics. You are pretty fed up with all the faddish theories of the day, but you have found comfort in neo-Marxist and political-economy frameworks that look at the importance of systemic change. In fact, one of your goals is to get beyond the influences of so many "rational" theories of organization and find new ways of thinking. In terms of implementation, you are dedicated to seeing the big picture and to grounding that big picture in real-world experiences that your staff encounter every day.

You are dedicated to promoting a justice perspective in the implementation process. Therefore, you often ask questions about diversity, the need for alternative approaches, and compliance with the principles of the NASW Code of Ethics. You advocate for alternative ways of evaluating any change or implementation process so that all voices are heard. You refer to values constantly, always trying to keep the group focused on the importance of understanding and dealing with value conflicts over what needs to be done. Sometimes you feel that yours is a lonely road and that you are not being heard, but you persist because you believe that justice must be served.

Questions to Guide the Debriefing

1. How does a person's position in an organization affect their perspectives on problem definition and problem solving?
2. What do aspects of each role and the position taken by the holder of the role demonstrate about social work practice?
3. What additional perspective(s) could or should be represented in this situation?

Organization-Practice Exercise 13

Agency Reorganization

This is an exercise in understanding organizational decision making, requiring some work on the front end. Three groups will be needed to participate in looking at three possible organizing formats.

1) Current structure group
2) Centralization group
3) Decentralization group

Each group has been assigned by their employer (The Foresight and Wisdom Social Planning and Administration Consultants Group, Inc.) as consultants to the agency to help it select an appropriate organizational form. The agency has presented their current organizational chart and two alternative organizational forms (centralization and decentralization). You have been asked for advice on: 1) an evaluation of the structure to which you are assigned, and 2) detailed justification for why this approach is appropriate to agency goals and objectives.

The Agency

The Elder Services Agency is a new community agency established to serve the aged. It is a spin-off of the Family Service Agency as a result of growing concern for the problems and needs of the aged population. It receives funding from various sources, including community donations, the United Way (13% of operating budget), foundations, business and labor groups, and federal grants from the state Agency on Aging under the Older American's Act.

Based on a community-needs assessment, the annual budget provides for the following services: 1) emergency financial assistance; 2) homemaker assistance; 3) housing, relocation, and emergency shelter; 4) legal aid and ombudsperson services; 5) employment counseling and placement; 6) recreational and educational programs; 7) vacation services, trips, charters; and 8) case management with referrals to other social agencies.

Services are provided through a centralized structure headed by an executive director, who is supported by an assistant director. The organizational chart reflects this structure.

The executive director is responsible for managing the agency, with the assistant director supervising the provision of social services through the social work staff. Initially, there were only the executive director, the chief accountant, and the social work and clerical staffs. Only counseling, information, and referral services were offered. Expansion of services necessitated the appointment of an assistant director—a trained social worker with a gerontology specialty who could directly supervise the delivery of services. The agency continued to grow, thus requiring additional staff. The assistant director became more involved in administrative matters while also continuing to assist the staff as service problems arose. Problems ranged from inadequate physical facilities to the provision of services to those unable to come to the office. The challenges proved to be more than the assistant director could handle. One of the experienced case workers was promoted to a supervisory position to assist staff with service problems and provide more clinical supervision. The assistant director then became even more involved in administrative and fund-raising matters, with the supervisor becoming the liaison between the staff and the administration.

Policies and procedures were formalized in an effort to gain order and effectively achieve established objectives. Communication became more formal and vertical, that is, from the client to the social work staff, through the supervisor to the administrative level, and vice versa. Coordination and communication was facilitated by history. All the key employees had worked together for some time and had helped to create the new organizational structure.

The number of clients has continued to increase and the agency's understanding of the need has also expanded. Families of clients have now become an integral part of service delivery. With the increasing need

CURRENT ORGANIZATIONAL CHART

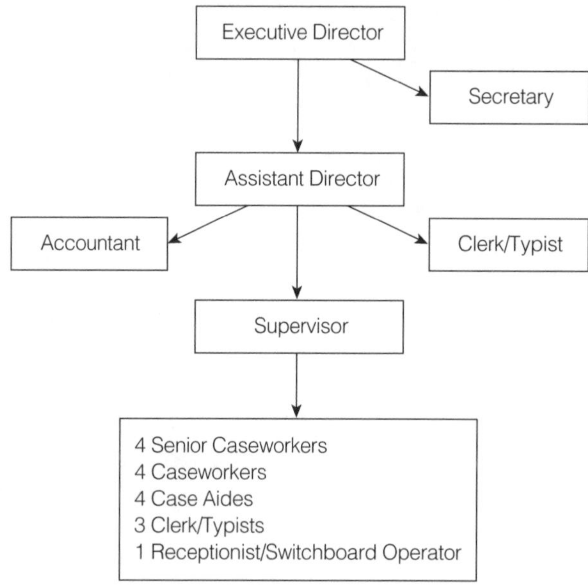

for service, administration has become more complex and demanding on the people holding the administrative positions.

Current Problems and Temporary Solutions

The expansion process has magnified old problems as this relatively young agency looks once again to modify its organizational structure. The caseworkers who feel the impact of increased client need for services are complaining. They are each handling a caseload of 50 and some have more. The case aides assigned to information and referral services are forced to provide counseling, for which they are not trained. The workers complain of time-consuming home visits they make to aged people in different neighborhoods. Travel takes half of the time of direct service provision, and workers are expected to see as many clients as possible. The supervisor has little time to supervise on a regular basis. Clerical staff experience problems in completing monthly statistical reports.

Organizational problems have been identified in the following areas: the span of control is more than the supervisor can handle; coordination of workers and workloads is difficult; unclear job definition and expectations create morale problems. As a result, services are deteriorating.

These problems have forced the agency to review the organizational structure. Suggestions for change include recruitment of additional trained workers interested in work with the aged; formulation of clear position descriptions for social workers and case aides; increased appropriations for maintenance of the agency; development of facilities for the aged in need of specialized services such as housing, assisted living, and the like.

Certain temporary steps can be taken to enable the agency to continue in operation. These ameliorate some major problems of the workers but do not help with the increased demands of clients. The discomfort among social work and clerical staff can be relieved by limiting intake and emphasizing referrals. A senior caseworker is being promoted to a second supervisory position, equally dividing the number of caseworkers and case aides between two supervisors. A weekly seminar has been conducted to train case aides and equip them with skills, and a seminar for casework staff is to be conducted.

Suggested Organization Structures

In order to meet the problems on a longer-range basis, two different structures have been developed and are to be considered. One would maintain the present centralized structure with four additional supervisory units, each providing a specialized service based on various client needs. (See the diagram of the centralized organization that follows.)

This type of organization offers both advantages and disadvantages. While it allows for a cluster of related services within a division, and provision of services through clearly defined categories, it does not reflect the fact that individuals may need a combination of services from various divisions. Overlapping and duplication of work is likely to occur, and coordination may be difficult. A unified, concerted effort is lost, and there is a possibility of "passing over" of responsibility for individual clients who may require more than one type of service. A client in need of multiple services may not establish a working relationship with any one worker. On the other hand, in this structure good internal communication may be effectively achieved, as can adequate span of control and minimization of distance between organizational levels.

The alternate solution is a decentralized system based on geographic units in neighborhood communities, through which clients may be readily reached. (See the diagram of the decentralized organization that follows.)

In the decentralized structure, each area office is a miniature Elder Services Agency, operating within a particular neighborhood. An advantage is that it allows for an individualized approach to the problems presented by the clients in the area. The services are likely to suit the community-related needs of clients, and the structure allows some flexibility in achieving agency objectives in each neighborhood.

This structure, however, requires significant effort in achieving agreement on procedures and policies. Flexibility and adaptability may be difficult to accommodate. Communication is likely to be difficult and characterized by conflict resulting from neighborhood orientation. The fact that what may work in one area may not necessarily work in another may limit cooperation in policy formation.

PROPOSED CENTRALIZED ORGANIZATION

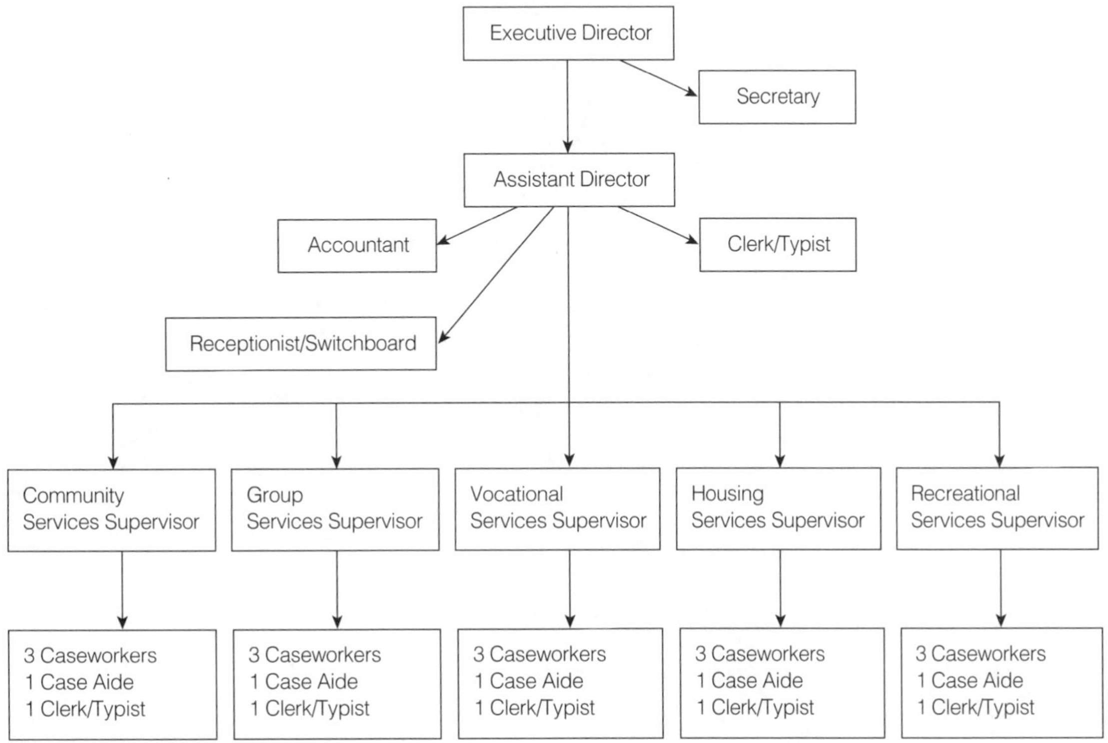

PROPOSED DECENTRALIZED ORGANIZATION

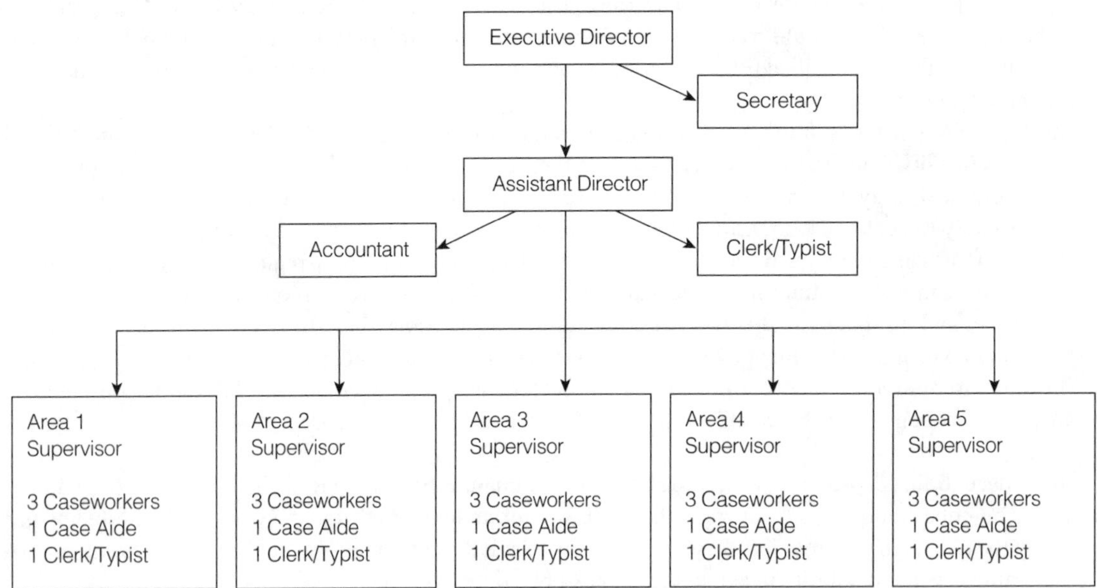

Organization-Practice Exercise 14

Neighborhood House

A new director of Neighborhood House is about to arrive (read the case description that follows this introduction for more information). You are staff members at Neighborhood House who have agreed to see if consensus might be reached on organization problems that should be addressed. You are committed to bettering the agency, its clients, and your profession. You know that with a new director coming in, this is a prime time to work for needed organization changes. You decide to develop a work plan, following the steps below.

Step 1: Prepare an intervention hypothesis. You recall that an intervention hypothesis contains both "if" and "then" parts, which are associated in a cause and effect relationship that proposes a relationship between a specific intervention and a desired result.

Step 2: Write a goal, then write at least one outcome objective, one process objective, and one set of activities. You recall that goals are broad statements of future or desired states that address the problem; that objectives include a time frame, a target, a result, and a results measurement criterion which lead to goal accomplishment, while activities are steps to be accomplished to achieve objectives.

Step 3: Decide on a strategy. Determine what strategy you will use for implementing your work plan. How would you go about setting the plan in motion, given that the new director is arriving?

The Neighborhood House Scenario

Introduction

Neighborhood House is located just outside the downtown area of a large industrial city of 800,000. For 100 years this agency has served a neighborhood populated originally by Eastern European immigrants but which is now largely African American. The agency founders established a liberal tradition and were eager to help newcomers enter the mainstream of American life. The agency did this very well for many years.

The Physical Environment

The agency is located in the midst of a low-cost housing project, composed of several low-rise buildings with about 500 families, or 2,500 people. Another, smaller housing project is several blocks away. In the area surrounding the housing projects the homes are multiple-family, wood-frame buildings, some with stores on the first floor. There is a limited number of brick apartment dwellings, which are very overcrowded, and people are also living in basements and empty stores. Some large industry is scattered throughout the area and there are some small manufacturing plants and auto-repair garages and junkyards. Railroad tracks and a freight yard bound the south side of the area. There is a large number of commercial and service stores—luncheonettes, candy stores, restaurants, beauty parlors, barbershops, and dry cleaners, as well as numerous bars and taverns. Large supermarkets do not exist in the area, but there are small independent groceries and meat markets.

The neighborhood is bounded on the north by a major four-lane street with a divider of concrete in some sections and grass in others separating the east- and west-flowing traffic. The southern boundary is marked by a rail line. Eastern and western boundaries are irregular and somewhat ill defined, but both tend to be recognized by physical features—a drainage canal on the east and an abandoned trolley line on the west. Two bus lines serve the area, one going to the downtown business and shopping district of the city that is not far away, and the other running across town. Many people work as domestics in residential sections of the city and others go to large industries. Most people have to use two different bus lines to get to work.

The Social Environment

There are two public elementary schools near the project, and a junior high across the street. These schools have small, inadequate playgrounds. There are also two parochial schools with playgrounds. A swimming pool is located across from one of the elementary schools. It is closed from 2:00 p.m.–4:00 p.m. every day for cleaning, and it closes at 8:00 p.m., making life more difficult in the heat of the summer. There is a well-baby clinic, a hospital within easy reach, and a medical center not far away. The League for Children, the Family Service Agency, and Catholic Charities are not far away in another neighborhood, but they usually offer only appointment times between 9:00 a.m. and 5:00 p.m.

Families have more than the usual share of social problems. Teachers at the local elementary schools estimate that 50 percent of the children have one parent absent. A number of children carry door keys, and many eat their lunches at candy stores in the neighborhood. There is considerable transience, with 327 transfer outs and 325 transfers into the local elementary schools during the year, out of a total of 1,871 children. Truancy is an ever-present problem in the public schools. It is less prevalent in the Catholic schools. The public schools are overcrowded, and for a while it was thought half-day sessions would be necessary. Some efforts to give special help include a school-lunch program used by about 40 percent of school children, one full-time social worker, tutoring in reading and math, and a program to induce teenagers to stay in school. The Board of Education conducts an after-school recreation program at the playgrounds.

Strangely, there are no major denominational churches in the area other than the Catholic church. There are two very small "store front" evangelical sects on the busy northern boundary street.

The crime rate is not generally publicized, although the precinct station is reputed to be the second busiest in the city. Violence-related death is twice that of the city's overall rate and there is a similar discrepancy for infant mortality. Almost half of the illegitimate births for the city are from this district. Public assistance figures are relatively low, perhaps because so many mothers are working.

A Youth Aid Bureau has done a rather good job attempting to understand and prevent juvenile delinquency. Two thirds of the juvenile cases for the whole city originate from this district, although it contains just 20 percent of the total population. The majority of the offenses involve taking things—larceny, assault, auto theft, and burglary. Drug dealing, while slow to develop, seems to be on the rise.

The Agency

Neighborhood House occupies a relatively new building in the midst of the housing project. It contains three offices, a conference room, one large multipurpose room that can be divided into three sections, a group activity room, and a kitchen. A county park about eight miles away is used for summer day camp. The agency bus is used for transportation to and from the park. A basement of one of the project buildings is assigned to the agency for use by the preschool program. Building code and day-care regulations restrict the program to 40 children. The playground next to Neighborhood House is staffed for limited hours by the Board of Education's Recreation Department. No lights are provided, and in the summer, teenagers flock into the building at dark.

Agency programs consist of: 1) preschool serving 110 children per year, 2) day camp serving about 150 children within an eight-week summer period, 3) after-school group activities serving about 130 elementary school children and 75 teenagers each day, 4) a tenant's association, and 5) family counseling done by a skillful and experienced case worker on a half-time basis, helping about 55 families a year with a variety of problems.

Until this year, the staff has consisted of a director, a program activities supervisor, one group-work supervisor, three group facilitators, a half-time case worker, a few volunteers from the colleges in the city, and four preschool staff, including the preschool coordinator. The program activities supervisor, the group work supervisor, and the half-time case worker reported to the director, and each, in turn, supervised the staff assigned to their areas. The staff are diverse, reflecting different ethnic, racial, and religious backgrounds.

The Neighborhood House budget has remained relatively stable for a number of years now, without drastic budget cuts but also with little or no increase. Two thirds of the budget comes from the United Way for specific programs, specifically the preschool program, the after-school program, and the day camp. At the present time the United Way favors programs in its member agencies that serve either disadvantaged youth or high-risk, vulnerable elders. The other third of the budget comes from limited camp and preschool fees and from money and special donations raised by board members. There is no endowment or reserve fund. There is a line-item budget, and most staff members have never seen this annual document.

Recently the United Way postponed making a scheduled quarterly allocation of funds to some agencies, including Neighborhood House. This happened because a high percentage of United Way pledge payments (in which donors had pledged to give money in partial payments made throughout the year or by monthly payroll deductions) were not being fulfilled. Corporate mergers, downsizing, and moves of corporate employees to other corporate locations out of town were blamed for this. As a result of the delayed allocation, the director of Neighborhood House has had enough and has just resigned. The group-work supervisor is working three quarters time due to this temporary budget reduction, which no one, including the board, wants, but which is unavoidable given the reduction.

The Board of Directors

There are sixteen board positions, including the president, treasurer, secretary, vice president, and immediate past president. Liberal, humanitarian values motivate the current board, just as they did the founders 100 years ago. The board is quite representative of the city as a whole, but is less representative of the Neighborhood House neighborhood. The board members are eager to be a force in improving social conditions in the city. Membership on the board carries some prestige among liberal minded, well-to-do persons in the community, and board membership is very stable, with little turnover. In the past five years, there have been only three new appointments to the board.

Neighborhood House and The Future

Historically, Neighborhood House has been effective but staff members are coming to recognize that problems in the neighborhood and the entire urban area are beginning to overwhelm the agency's ability to help community members cope. They know that there are problems—that there are underserved clients and potential clients in the community who could be helped, that there is confusion in the community and in the agency about personnel and agency functions as a result of the agency not having a mission statement, and that a resource development plan is needed, given the current situation of declining resources. There is an undercurrent present among staff to the effect that some employees who have been with the agency for a number of years feel less involved in agency planning and programming than in "the old days." While over the years many staff members have moved on from Neighborhood House to better positions in other agencies throughout the community, it is reported that, more than usual, many résumés of current staff are showing up in other agencies in the city and county.

Organization-Practice Activities

Organization-Practice Activity A

Know Your Agency

Complete the following survey about a social-service organization you are familiar with. Interview appropriate agency personnel and review agency records and documents in order to answer the following questions.

1. Name and address of the agency:

____

____

2. In what year was the agency established? ________________________

3. What are the functions of the agency?

____

____

____

____

4. Who does it serve?

____

____

____

____

5. Under what auspices does the agency operate?

   Governmental ________________________

   Not-for-profit—Is it secular or faith-based?________________________

   For profit________________________

6. On what geographical level does the agency operate?

   ____Local

   ____State

   ____National

   ____International

   ____Other

7. What is the catchment or service area of the agency?

____

____

8. How did the agency originate?

_____Established by statute

_____Established by voluntary association of interested persons

_____Established by some other organization (a spin-off)

_____By bequest

_____By merger

_____By federation

_____ Other ______________________________

9. Either locate an organizational chart or draw one.

10. In relation to the structure and processes of the agency:

What or who is the group or individual with ultimate control?

____

____

Is there a membership? What are the qualifications for membership?

____

____

Is there a board? What is it called? Is it directive (policy-determining) or advisory? By whom is it elected or appointed?

____

____

____

Who appoints the executive?

____

____

What major departments are there, if any?

____

____

____

____

What districts or branches are there, if any?

____

____

11. What document(s) is the source of administrative authority for the agency?

_____Law

_____Executive order

_____Charter (papers of incorporation)

_____Constitution

_____Bylaws

_____Other______________________________________

12. By whom was this document adopted or promulgated?

____

13. What topics does this document cover?

____

____

14. How can the document be amended or revised?

____

____

15. Is the agency:

_____A branch of any other local, state, or national agency?

_____A member of a United Way or other funding federation?

_____A member of a community-welfare council or council of agencies?

16. What are the major sources of funding for the agency?

____

____

____

____

____

____

17. Give approximate figures for the following:

_______________Current budget or total expenditures for last fiscal year

Number of staff positions divided according to administrative, professional, clerical, and other categories

____

____

____

Number of all staff authorized and number of positions filled

____

____

18. What are roles for social workers?

_____Direct service

_____ Management

_____Administration

_____Other

Organization-Practice Activity B

Organizational Categories

Whether they are public, nonprofit, or for profit, organizations are often committed to or have allegiances to other organizations and to other arenas. Relationships with other groups and organizations may mean an organization is involved in associations, coalitions, alliances, collaborations, and so forth. Affiliations may be formed around ideologies, beliefs, values, or population groups. Some of the relationships are more explicit than others. Using your field agency or an organization in which you are employed:

1. Categorize the organization by its associations, affiliations (as in ideological communities), host relationships, and/or other relationships. Justify why you have made the categorization(s) you have.

   Associations

   Affiliations

   Host relationships (where either your organization is the "host" or is "hosted by" another organization)

   Other relationships

2. Assess the quality of the connections. Are they easy fits or is there a forced relationship?

3. What are the implications of the organization's relationships specified above? Speculate about how these connections (or lack of same) impede or enhance service delivery.

____

____

____

____

4. Are there groups, other organizations, or communities with which the organization needs to develop relationships? If so, list them below:

____

____

____

____

Organization-Practice Activity C

Organizational Cultural Competence

Cross (1988)[1] has developed a cultural competence continuum for human-service agencies that moves from cultural destructiveness to cultural competence. Using the definitions that follow, assess an agency you are familiar with to determine where it fits on the continuum.

Cultural destructiveness: Assumes one culture is superior and should eliminate other cultures for the good of all.

Cultural incapacity: Is not intentionally destructive, but through ignorance and incompetence not only does not value difference, but also may limit or harm minorities through action or inaction.

Cultural blindness: Believes that color and culture make no difference, thus ignoring cultural strengths, encouraging assimilation, and blaming victims for their problems.

Cultural precompetence: Recognizes challenges in responding to minority persons and makes attempts to improve abilities, but may lack information or skills in how to proceed.

Cultural competence: Accepts and respects differences, paying close attention to the dynamics of difference and seeks to expand knowledge of cultures and their strengths and resources.

1. Where do you think your agency fits?

____

____

____

____

2. Provide evidence for why you have categorized it as you have.

____

____

____

____

3. What specific recommendations would you make in order to improve its current level of cultural competence?

____

____

____

____

[1]Cross, T. L. (1988). Cultural competence continuum. *Focal Point, 3* (1). [Bulletin of the Research and Training Center to Improve Services for Seriously Emotionally Handicapped Children and Their Families. Regional Institute for Human Services, School of Social Work, Portland State University, Oregon.]

4. What are positive or negative consequences, for the organization and for the members, of your answer in #3?

____

____

____

____

Organizational-Practice Activity D

Program Assessment

Select a proposed service-delivery program that you would like to see implemented. Using what you know about that program, consider the following questions to guide your in-class dialogue about the program.

Program History & Intent

1. What is the intent of this program?
2. How did it come about? For example, is this program being implemented because it has just been mandated through public policy? What is its history?
3. Will the program lead to large-scale change?
4. Are there internal contradictions within this program?
5. Are there theories or assumptions that guide this program? If so, can you identify them?

Resources and Oversight

6. Who will implement this program?
7. Who will monitor and evaluate this program?
8. Who will establish administrative rules or oversight for this program?
9. How many resources will be needed for this program?
10. Will there be multiple funding streams?
11. Will professionals, paraprofessional staff, and volunteers be needed?

Host Organization

12. What organization is involved in the implementation of this program? What do you know about its commitment to and agendas for this program?
13. What organizational leaders support or oppose this program?
14. Who are the supervisors and administrative staff who will be involved in this program? Do they oppose or support the program?
15. How do direct practice staff view this program and what are the implications of their views? Do they understand this program? Are they committed to its implementation?
16. How will consumers/clients view this program?
17. How will consumer/client interactions with staff influence the course of this program? How will they be involved in program implementation?
18. How will other groups and organizations collaborate with the host organization to implement this program? Will outside partners be needed, and if so, for what purposes?

Internal Implementation

19. Is the program innovation clearly communicated and explained to implementing staff so that they are familiar with its goals and objectives?
20. Are staff clear about their roles in implementing this program?
21. Is someone in the organization responsible for troubleshooting when problems develop in program implementation?

22. Is orientation and in-service training provided to staff so that they will have appropriate skills to implement this program?
23. Is implementation of the innovation built into staff promotion and performance review?
24. Do staff receive bonuses and other rewards for additional work on the program?
25. Are new staff to be hired to perform key tasks in the program?
26. Do executives in the host organization demonstrate strong leadership in monitoring and trouble-shooting?
27. Will the host organization be able to either allocate or locate new resources dedicated to implementing and developing the program as they are needed?

External Considerations

28. Are collaborative relationships with external organizations in place as needed for program implementation?
29. Are appropriate outreach and community-education processes being initiated?
30. What people, groups, and organizations in the larger environment are lined up to support this implementation process?
31. What type of public relations materials need to be developed?
32. What are the negative and positive contextual factors that need to be considered as the program is implemented?
33. Are there board or advisory-council members that need to be added, given this program's implementation?

Program Evaluation

34. How will the program be evaluated?
35. Who will conduct the evaluation?
36. What mechanisms are in place (or need to be in place) in order to use evaluation data to redesign the program as needed?

Organization-Practice Activity E

Funding One's Program

A program can be well designed but it requires resources to make it come alive. Sometimes those resources are minimal and can be provided within current budgets as long as a board of directors or governing body approves the allocation. However, most creative programming will likely require a funding source or sources that go beyond current budgetary allowances. When this is the case, someone has to investigate funding options while a program is being designed.

No matter whether the potential funder is a local United Way agency, a government agency, or a private foundation, one must demonstrate to that source that a program is worth funding.

Step 1: Select a service-delivery area in which you are going to be developing programs, or a particular target population in which your field agency or place of employment is interested. Go to the Web and locate advocacy groups concerned with this area or target population, and find out what sources are funding them.

Step 2: If you are seeking grant monies, but don't know where to start, there are directories for almost every purpose. Note that directories were once found on reference library shelves, but now one can access them on line as well. If you are looking for government funding sources, note that there are directories that can guide you to federal funding for drug-prevention programs or to National Institute on Health (NIH) grants and contracts. There are entire books of potential funding resources. Go to a Web site (such as The Foundation Center's at www.fdncenter.org) and locate a directory of potential funding sources for a program in your area of interest.

Step 3: Funders often feel somewhat overwhelmed with the number of applications they receive. Both funders and potential grantees want to know that there is a "fit" between their funding goals and a proposed program. Both parties stand to benefit by knowing if a program does not fit with a funding source's goals. Therefore, some funders will seek preproposals—much shorter versions of an entire program plan—that can give the potential funder a chance to encourage or discourage submission of a full application. Locate a request for a letter of inquiry or preproposal from a funding source that might be interested in a population group with which you are familiar.

Step 4: If you know what funding source to which you are going to apply, there will be a set of proposal or application guidelines, often called a Request for Proposal (RFP). Locate a copy of an RFP.

Step 5: Agencies that partner with the United Way have to prepare budget requests each year. In recent years, the United Way has been very interested in outcome-based performance measures. Locate information for prospective grantees from your local United Way agency.

1. What have you learned about the process of examining possible funding sources?

____

____

____

2. Were there any surprises?

____

____

3. How might you use this information to get a proposal funded?

____

____

4. What questions do you still have?

____

____

____

____

5. Now assume that you are a project manager of a rather large social service agency and have been tasked with the responsibility of determining an appropriate funding stream for the new children's service program that the agency is developing. A thorough needs assessment was conducted that led the board to determine that mental-health services for preschool children would be the next program to be developed. They have asked you to determine whether either a government or foundation grant or a contract would be the better way to go. How would you begin?

____

____

____

____

Organization-Practice Activity F

The Political–Economic Context

Locate an annual report from an organization you are familiar with and look at the revenues and expenditures for that year. This could be your field agency or a place of employment. Use the following questions to see what you can determine about the political–economic context of funding.

Note that there may be questions you cannot answer, given the detail (or lack of detail) in the annual report. See if you can find anyone who can talk with you about these questions. If not, make notes about questions you can't find information about and think about why this information might not be readily available.

1. How have decisions about the budget been made in the past?
2. Have there been changes in leadership that have shaped things differently from previous years?
3. Has the source of authority shifted (for example, from national to state)?
4. Are there cultural norms surrounding the budget?
5. Is the budget viewed as something magical/untouchable for staff?
6. Who will be included in the budgetary process?
7. What role does the governing board play in approving the budget (as rubberstamp or as experts)?
8. Is there Advisory Council, staff, consumer, or other input that goes into the budgetary process? What assumptions will those persons bring to the budgeting process?
9. What is the breakdown of revenues in your organization by:

   - Client fees
   - Third-party payments
   - Contracts
   - Fund-raising activities
   - United Way grants
   - Private grants
   - Public grants
   - Contributions
   - Endowments
   - Other

10. What is the major funding source? What are the implications of this being the major funder?
11. How have those sources changed over time?
12. How does your agency determine the line items of expenditures?
13. Can you tell what is valued by examining what amount is allocated to each item?
14. What funding sources will be approached for future resources?
15. What interests do these sources represent?
16. How does the agency frame what they do in order to target funding sources? Do they alter their strategies, depending on which source is targeted? And if yes, how?
17. What constraints are imposed by those who control the revenues?
18. Are there regulations and/or standards that are tied to funding?
19. Are there political ideologies tied to funding?
20. How much does your organization pay/reward personnel?
21. Are adequate benefits budgeted for staff?
22. If volunteers are used in your organization, are their efforts calculated into the cost per output, per outcome?

23. Does your organization invest in a paid volunteer coordinator?
24. Are in-kind contributions considered part of the organization's budget?
25. How does your agency figure indirect costs? How equitable is that calculation for different programs/ services?
26. Have corners been cut? How has cutting those corners affected staff, clients, and others?

Organization-Practice Activity G

Evergreen Agency Memo

Writing for organizational purposes requires the ability to communicate succinctly yet thoroughly. You must produce a written document that is jargon-free and sets a tone of believability and acceptance of the ideas being communicated. You must also keep in mind that organization employees receive numerous intra-organizational communications every day; yours should not get lost in the shuffle.

On the next page is an actual memorandum written by someone in a real organization; only the organization's name has been changed. Read it through and ask yourself about its succinctness, thoroughness, use of jargon, believability, and how likely the reader will be to accept the ideas presented. Then, rewrite the memo to improve it, using the criteria mentioned above.

EVERGREEN AGENCY

MEMORANDUM

TO: All Evergreen Agency Employees

FROM: Bill S. Spreader, Director of Human Resources

SUBJECT: Evergreen Agency's Work/Life Partnership

DATE: 00/00/00

"The Evergreen Agency Work/Life Partnership." No doubt you've heard the phrase, but do you know what it is? In broad terms, it refers to the programs, benefits, and policies established to support you in your efforts to manage work and personal responsibilities.

Evergreen Agency's Work/Life Partnership provides you with a wide range of resources as you strive to earn a living and live a rich, full life. It recognizes that you are being asked to work harder and smarter than ever before. It accepts that personal responsibilities can be complex and demanding, offering the potential for distress and distraction in the workplace. It also recognizes that, depending on your personal circumstances, you may have important concerns and needs related to work, personal, health, and financial issues.

Like all effective initiatives, *Evergreen Agency's Work/Life Partnership* will continuously evolve to meet the changing needs of employees. Evergreen Agency's Work/Life Council, formed in 1999, is comprised of employees who will continue to guide this evolution. The Council will provide input and direction regarding Evergreen Agency's current and future initiatives and assist the agency in identifying work/life issues that need to be examined.

A key priority for the Council will be to raise awareness among employees of the various work/life-related programs and services available to them. The brochure being developed will represent a first step toward that end. It is being designed as a concise reference tool to highlight the scope of programs Evergreen Agency offers and to place important phone numbers at your fingertips. You may need some services only once, while others may be used on a regular basis, such as HelpPsych's personal convenience services (HelpServeConnect).

In addition, EAP sites have been added to the Work/Life channel on Evergreen Agency's intranet (EAN) to provide you with easy access to information about the many services available to you and your family.

The Council is committed to the continued enhancement of Evergreen Agency's work/life initiatives. Additional priorities for this year include the integration of work/life issues into management and business practices. We invite your feedback and recommendations for work/life solutions that will benefit the people of Evergreen Agency and ensure Evergreen Agency continues to meet its objectives.

Organization-Practice Activity H

Strategic-Planning Analysis

Ask to see a copy of the strategic plan for an organization you are familiar with. Use the following framework to analyze the plan.

1. What goals for the organization are included in this plan? How do they serve as a guide for the rest of the strategic plan?
2. What are the objectives in the plan? Does the plan distinguish between process and outcome objectives?
3. Review the objectives to determine if they have each of these components:

   A. Time frame
   B. Target of change
   C. Results to be achieved
   D. Criteria for documenting, monitoring, and measuring change

4. Would you rewrite any of the objectives or are they clear enough?
5. Are there tasks or activities that flesh out the process objectives? Do they have these parts:

   A. Date due
   B. Person or persons responsible
   C. Task to be completed

6. Does this strategic plan make sense in light of what you know about this organization?
7. Is there attention to context and to political and economic feasibility?
8. What would you change about this strategic plan if you were asked to consult with this agency?

Organization-Practice Activity I

Evaluability Assessment

From your field agency or place of employment, locate a program-evaluation plan, or alternatively, the agency's management information system (MIS). You may need to interview the person(s) in charge of the evaluation or the maintenance of the information system in order to answer the following:

1. Can the program evaluation or the MIS be adequately carried out as planned, with due regard for maintenance of personal rights and integrity?
2. Could any harm come to the program, or to the agency's clients or personnel as a result of the functioning of the MIS or the evaluation process?
3. Is it reasonable to expect the cooperation of clients and/or personnel in the monitoring and evaluation processes?
4. In what ways might the evaluation or MIS be dysfunctional to human performance?
5. Who may gain or lose from the evaluation findings?
6. From this analysis, would you suggest any changes in order to make the program evaluable? Should an evaluation proceed? Why? If not, why not?

Organization-Practice Activity J

Sunnyview In-Basket

The following is an in-basket activity that provides an opportunity to examine items that might come to a person in a professional position and to figure out how to deal with these items. The purpose of this activity is to stimulate your abilities to respond to organizational and human problems in organizations in a timely manner. These documents are challenging and fun, as well as representative of the type of items that come across a social work macro practitioner's desk. You may complete these activities as a group in class or individually outside of class.

The Setting

Sunnyview is a nonprofit 162-bed skilled-care facility, affiliated with the United Methodist Church. There are currently 155 residents; 93 are female and 62 are male. The majority of the residents are Caucasian (70%), 20% are African American, and 10% are Hispanic. Eighty percent of the residents are Protestant, 10% are Catholic, 7% Jewish, and 3% have no religious affiliation. The average mean age is 81, with an age range from 25 to 102.

Because Sunnyview was established by the United Methodist Church in 1909 as a home for retired pastors and their widows, there is a long tradition of using volunteers. The volunteer program has expanded over the years and includes interested citizens from various religious and secular groups. During holiday seasons, volunteers have a special role in organizing events, decorating, and scheduling various activities.

The home is located in Crystal Town. The time is the present. The characters are discussed below.

Organization of the Home

You are the executive director of Sunnyview; you have been promoted recently to this position. An associate director (Jim Wilson, who was promoted into your old position) supervises a director of nursing services (Jean Smith, a clinical nurse specialist by training), a business manager (Joe Montoya), a social worker/activity director (Jane Wade), and a facilities engineer (John Tyler). Together with you, the executive director, each of these persons participates in Sunnyview's administrative team and supervises the staff persons in their respective departments. The staff is made up of an assortment of professionals, paraprofessionals, maintenance workers, and volunteers. For example, floor nurses are professional R.N.s and L.P.N.s; paraprofessionals include nurse's aides, dietary/kitchen staff, maintenance, and housekeeping personnel. A cadre of approximately 20 volunteers is overseen by the social worker/activity coordinator.

The associate director is a Caucasian male. The director of nursing and the social worker are Caucasian females. The facilities engineer is an African-American male, and the business manager, also male, is Hispanic. The nurse's aides, dietary, engineering, and housekeeping staff are 80% female. Seventy-five percent of the paraprofessional staff are people of color.

Your Role

Recently, you were promoted from associate director to be the executive director of Sunnyview. You have an M.S.W. and your nursing home administration license. You have furthered your education by attending continuing-education workshops. Most recently, you attended the American Institute for Managing Diversity. You have been working as executive director for about one month.

Your Day

You have just entered your office on a beautiful, sunny Tuesday morning in the fall and as you expected, you find a number of items in your in basket, voice-mail messages, and e-mail messages. You were at a nursing home regulations conference last week, and Monday was a holiday. Now, as you have your first cup of coffee, you are trying to sort through your in-basket to determine what you will need to do first, and for the rest of the day.

Please do the following:

1. Look over the items in your in-basket (contained in the pages that follow) in order to see what is awaiting you.

2. Devise a plan for the day, listing items in order, ranked according to their importance. Do this on one page.

___

___

___

___

___

___

___

3. Write the three items you would address first, second, and third below:

Item 1 ___

Item 2 ___

Item 3 ___

4. Then, discuss why you prioritized as you did in questions 2 and 3 above. Do this by identifying and listing organizing or guiding principle(s) that emerged in your process, and by listing any decision-making criteria you used.

Guiding principles that emerged:

___

___

___

___

___

Decision-making criteria used: ___

___

___

___

___

5. Address the item that appears at the top of your priority list and present your rationale for why it is at the top of the list, and think about your plan for it. If the item requires an oral response, such as a telephone call, in one page or less, write what you and the other party would say to one another. If the item may be answered by e-mail or by memo, in one page or less, write the actual e-mail or letter you would send.

In-Basket Item A

SUNNYVIEW NURSING HOME

"Where every day is a sunny day."

MEMORANDUM

TO: Executive Director

FROM: Managing Diversity Task Force

RE: Next Steps

DATE: (Today's date)

The Task Force on Managing Diversity has now met three times, and we have come to believe that this agency must get beyond rhetoric and take some action. Although we feel that affirmative-action strategies have been used fairly effectively in the past, this agency must move toward a more contemporary response to diversity issues.

We need your advice on what next steps we need to take, particularly in relation to gender differences. We are meeting this afternoon at 4:00 and would appreciate having suggestions to consider at this meeting.

In-Basket Item B

SUNNYVIEW NURSING HOME
"Where every day is a sunny day."

MEMORANDUM

TO: Executive Director

FROM: President, Board of Directors

RE: Policy on Religious Holidays

DATE: (Today's date)

As you know, four of our employees are Jewish. They have asked to leave early on Friday for a Jewish holiday. They wish to prepare for it. We are a United Methodist agency, but it seems we should accommodate their request. One problem, however, is a special meeting of the Board of Directors to which staff are invited to present information on their programs. Three of these employees are needed at that meeting. As you know, we have had problems in the past with staff attendance at this meeting, and the Board is anxious to hear from all managerial staff. The Board itself has three members who are Jewish. Do you have a suggestion as to how we should handle this?

In-Basket Items C–I

When you access your electronic mail system, you receive these messages:

C. I need to talk with you as soon as possible about a medical leave. This is very personal so I need to talk with you confidentially. Can we get together today? Jean (director of nursing)

D. Gee, I'm glad you are back! Did you know that Jean (the director of nursing) is considering taking a medical leave? Before you talk to her, we need to talk. Jim (associate director)

E. I was just going over our financial report for the month and I see there are some discrepancies in how we are handling compensatory time. We need to clarify this policy because I think we are in danger of overpaying some of our staff. Joe (business manager)

F. Hey, where have you been? I've been trying to contact you for days! Did you see that big spread in the paper about how nursing homes are ripping off paraprofessional staff? Seems to me we need to write a rebuttal and get as many administrators involved as possible in the process. Can you come to an ad hoc meeting this Tuesday afternoon at the coalition office? (From the head of the local nursing home coalition group.)

G. I'm in the process of trying to decide how I'm going to fire a volunteer and I really need your advice. This volunteer is really dedicated but has some habits that are just not acceptable in a nursing home. To complicate it, this person also has been a big supporter, so I have to do this very carefully. I've really thought about this all weekend. When could we get together to talk? Jane (the social worker/activity coordinator)

H. The Athletic Committee meets Monday at 5:30 p.m. (for food) and 6:00 p.m. for the meeting. Can you be there? (From your club.)

I. Hey, I hope everything is going well. The plumber just called and can meet one of us at the house at 3:00 today to take care of that leak. I can't be there because I have a conference call coming in. Can you make it? Thanks! xx (From your significant other.)

In-Basket Item J

7036 Buttin Drive
New Town, USA 55555

Dear Executive Director:

I am a concerned citizen who is writing to let you know about a situation that greatly disturbs me. I'm not the kind of person who normally resorts to writing these type of letters, but I am to the point that I can no longer ignore this situation.

Two years ago we started a small adult care home for older persons who were in transition between home and nursing facility. Jane Wade, who is now your social worker, was our case manager at that time, and she was very kind and sensitive to both our situation as a new business and the older adults' needs. Last year, as we began our second year as an adult care home provider, Jane was replaced by a new social worker named Ann Jones.

Recently, we had some difficulties with one of our older residents, and it was not handled particularly well by Ms. Jones. As a result, my wife and I decided that we could no longer provide adult care. However, that is not why I'm writing because I know you have nothing to do with Ms. Jones or her work.

I am writing to tell you that it has come to our attention through mutual friends that this situation described in the preceding paragraph was not kept confidential. Apparently, some person or persons in your agency have communicated the difficulties we had to others in the community. This is a small community where neighbors know one another well. The fact that our business has been shared with others is beyond our comprehension. We had someone in our local church come up the other day and ask us about what happened, and this was someone we know only casually!

I am writing to you because this is a breach of confidentiality. Both Ms. Wade and Ms. Jones assured us that our business would always be kept in strictest confidence. The fact that this has not happened has harmed us greatly. We first went to our minister (Karl Smith of the First Episcopal Church) and asked him what to do. He said that we should let you know because this has the potential to harm your social worker's reputation and effectiveness in the community.

We hope you will be in touch with us very soon. We have always trusted your home to provide quality services and we know you will want to address this situation with your employee, Ms. Wade, immediately.

Sincerely,
Nigel Smith

In-Basket Item K

SUNNYVIEW NURSING HOME
"Where every day is a sunny day."

MEMORANDUM

TO: All Staff

FROM: Associate Director

RE: Suggestions for Enhancing Patient Autonomy

DATE: Last Friday's Date

As you know, there is a continual push by nursing home advocates to examine issues of autonomy and patient rights in long-term care. This movement has been spurred by recent reports of increased elder abuse in long-term care settings.

To some degree the decision to leave a private home and enter an institution necessitates compromise by residents, and might be seen as a negotiated trade: the facility provides assistance with tasks such as meals, hygiene, grooming, and medical attention that the individual is unable to manage privately; in return, the resident abides by policies and routines which enhance the general welfare of the facility "community." No one could argue that some compromise of personal rights is necessary in any group living situation. Moreover, since medical problems or physical or mental limitations nearly always motivate nursing home placement, it may even be legitimate to suggest that more compromise is necessary to ensure the medical stability, comfort, and safety of a community of relatively dependent people.

We are all overworked here and I know that each of you feels like one more demand will put you over the edge. However, we are committed to finding ways that we can enhance resident autonomy, to meet the directives of the law, and to prevent elder abuse at all costs. Therefore, I am asking that you submit your suggestions about how we might work toward these goals together. I look forward to having your input.

In-Basket Item L

Memo from a staff person in response to the associate director's memo to all staff of last Friday. This carries today's date and has just been received.

SUNNYVIEW NURSING HOME
"Where every day is a sunny day."

MEMORANDUM

To: Jim Wilson, Associate Director

From: Jane Wade, Social Worker/Activity Director

Re: Your memo

Date: (Today's date)

Thanks for asking me and my staff about resident autonomy and what might be done. We don't want to sound disrespectful, but it seems that all we ever talk about is how to please the state inspectors and that the only reason we are doing these things is to (CYA) cover ourselves. Maybe we're wrong, but this is how we feel. We are not abusing residents!

That minimum data set (MDS) form is just another example of how we have to please the state. We fill these out every day, but the nurses never refer to this information. So why are we doing this? The nurses use progress notes to keep track of patient condition and the MDS becomes just more paperwork to complete. What we learn today will likely be outdated in a few months.

Patient rights are posted in the appropriate places and we do periodic training so everyone knows what they mean. Realistically, residents don't always remember what we have said. We don't think this is a problem because staff are trained to know what the residents' rights are. We can remind them when things come up, and volunteers probably don't need to know this much information. It would only serve to confuse them.

As far as the training of aides is concerned, I think that is a good idea. These women don't have any formal education and many seem to carry their personal problems to work with them. This training provides them with information on how to be a little more professional. The problem we see is that the turnover rate is awfully high, making for limited consistency. Maybe we could find some incentives to keep those aides who are competent.

It seems to me that we need to do some thinking about how staff might feel better around here. The residents have it pretty good. It's the staff who are overworked and overextended. So my suggestion is that we do something for staff so they aren't feeling abused by the system!

cc: Executive Director

Part 5

Leadership and Professional Development

Key words:

campaign tactics
career planning
collaboration tactics
contest tactics
life-long learning
multicultural practice
social work leadership
self-awareness

Introduction

In the final section of this workbook, you will go beyond critical thinking, cultural competence, and ethical judgment to self-awareness, which is necessary for social work leadership. We think that by knowing your own assumptions and by thinking critically, and using the skills developed in social work education, all social workers can become valuable members of organizations and their communities. Social work core values and ethical principles must set the stage for social work leadership.

As in previous sections, we have organized leadership and professional development exercises and activities according to ascending levels of complexity. The chart that follows categorizes the material in this section by demystifying leadership, conceptualizing and defining leadership, increasing leadership sensitivity, practicing leadership-related tasks, and enhancing leadership change skills.

It is our strong belief that every educated social worker has leadership responsibilities in the setting in which they work and that every educated social worker has leadership potential. In this section of the workbook, we'll focus on developing the necessary attitudes about responsibility in an organization, based on professional skills and a set of values that compel individuals to act for the betterment of the organization and the clients it serves. You will see that from our perspective, formal authority is not required. What *is* required is motivation, along with knowledge, skills, and information for accurate decision making in determining that change is necessary. Through exercises and activities we hope you will develop your vision of what information is important to gather and when to share it so change can happen. We expect those using this workbook to go beyond just identifying and assessing problems and move toward identifying and facilitating successful problem solution. Here you will develop collaboration, campaign, and contest tactics for change, because social work is a change-oriented profession and social workers should lead in initiating change, regardless of their organizational role.

Self-awareness is the cornerstone to successful leadership, so here you will find opportunities to develop a consciousness about yourself, including personal expectations about work. You will develop an ability to manage boundaries to separate personal needs from the higher-order needs of clients and the organization. You will finish this section with an awareness of your strengths and vulnerabilities for without this, critical analysis will fall short of its potential. Additional work may help you uncover your personal biases, habitual distortions, personal behavior, and personal style so that you can choose a communication and leadership style most likely to succeed in any given situation.

In this section, you'll also go beyond the earlier discussions of cultural competence toward competent practice in multicultural environments. Exercises and activities will guide you through the stages of multicultural practice, including self-respect, dialogue, curiosity, a sense of safety, and recognition of worthiness. Because cultures, organizations, communities, and their problems change continuously, it is necessary to maintain competence through life-long learning.

This final section of the workbook closes with exercises and activities that will facilitate thinking about the development of your career after graduation. This includes consideration of leadership roles in the profession and in assisting clients. We include advice on searching for initial post-degree positions, along with exercises in career planning to assess current interests in particular populations and practice settings. We also provide activities guaranteed to engage you in life-long learning so that social work competencies can remain targeted and appropriate for responding to the needs of the times. We provide this with a wish for our readers' long and effective careers.

"The Days of Our Placements: Scene VI"

As the semester and academic year drew to a close, the students realized that complete victories are few and far between, but that partial victories can be good for all involved. A pilot after-school-care program for elementary school latch-key children was slated to begin operating at the agency the next fall. Support was to come from in-kind contributions from the agency (space and personnel), the school board (supplies and food), and parents (rotating volunteer recreational aides recruited from the community). The Nice Street project was not as clean in its outcome. There was a study commission at work, with construction halted until it reported. It turned out that the street, when it became one-way, would be the best route home for many downtown workers, including those in city hall. The role of the agency was still not clear, however; at last report the Community House Board Program Committee and Finance Committee were reviewing agency priorities in preparation for a board retreat and planning meeting. One thing was clear, however, and Harry had been right. Mission statements could change. The existing statement was so general and so wishy-washy that all agreed that something had to be done with it to maintain agency credibility.

The student group recognized that the year was drawing to a close and that they would be facing some personal changes. In a sense, some disengagement was beginning to take place. Things seemed more rushed and they spent less time interacting as a group. Maria and Harry seemed to be present less, often being off working together, rather than with the whole group. The field instructor was talking about things like "little successes" and "termination."

The group did face some problems. Chrystal, for example, complained that the substance-abuse program staff seemed to treat female clients with less regard than they did male clients. Yusof replied that perhaps, since she would be leaving the agency and would have little to lose, she could gather examples of this and point it out, maybe even proposing appropriate alternate ways of treating females. Chrystal gasped and said, "But I'm only a student." "Yeah, for about two more weeks is all," shot back Tamara. "Hey, it's show time!—time to be a social worker." After that exchange, you would have thought that the roof had fallen in—there was sudden silence, nervous glances, and then Yusof came back into the conversation, suggesting that maybe they could leave the agency with one last, good change. Everyone said, "Sure, ok, let's go for it." They decided Chrystal could take the lead, but all would work through the plan and be behind her all the way. That night they had a special meeting over coffee, at which they summarized their knowledge about change, and they began to formulate a plan of action. They also decided they really liked one another and wanted to continue their educational journey together by setting up their own shared Web site, planning a one-year reunion, and agreeing to be an employment self-help group as they sought jobs.

Leadership and Professional Development: Exercise and Activity Chart		
Focus	**Exercises**	**Activities**
Demystifying Leadership		Activity A: Providing Leadership
Conceptualizing and Defining Leadership	Exercise 1: Teamwork Definitions	Activity B: Macro-Practice Roles Activity C: Preferred Tactics
Increasing Leadership Sensitivity	Exercise 2: Theory and Leadership Exercise 3: Managing Differences Exercise 4: Organizational Assumptions	Activity D: Persuasive Leadership
Practicing Leadership-Related Tasks	Exercise 5: Ethical Leadership Exercise 6: Mentoring New Workers Exercise 7: Six-Month Evaluation	Activity E: Interviewing Outline
Enhancing Leadership Change Skills	Exercise 8: Interviewing Do's and Don'ts Exercise 9: Communication Inhibitors Exercise 10: Asking Questions Exercise 11: Team Analysis Exercise 12: Long-Term-Care Advocates	Activity F: Emergency Preparedness Activity G: Job Search

Leadership Exercises

Leadership Exercise 1

Teamwork Definitions

There are several concepts that are critical to participating on a team and providing leadership in one. As a group, discuss how you could define each of the following concepts and then share your definitions with the class. In class, compare and contrast the team products.

Team values and norms

____

____

Accommodating differences

____

____

Significant team communication

____

____

Conflict resolution

____

____

Decision making

____

____

Role definition

____

____

Team leadership

____

____

Responsibility

____

____

Power

____

____

Position and status

____

____

Supervision

____

____

Leadership Exercise 2

Theory and Leadership

During the first portion of class time, work by yourself to answer the following questions about theoretical approaches to understanding organizations. Then, as a group, compare your results in order to benefit from each other's ideas and knowledge about organizational theories.

The following is a list of some major theoretical approaches to structuring organizations and the behavior within them.

- Classical Organization Theory (Scientific Management Theory)
- Neoclassical Organization Theory (Behavioral Theory)
- Human Resource Theory (Organizational Behavior Theory, especially Maslow, McGregor's Theory X and Theory Y, and Likert's Participative Management)
- Modern Structural Organizational Theory
- Systems Theory
- Organization Culture Theory (including Sensemaking)
- Power and Politics Theory (including Feminist Theory)

1. Given the assumptions of each theoretical perspective, what might be the requirements for excellent human-service leadership in each? What would be expected of the organizational leader?

Theory	Leadership Requirements	Expectations of the Leader

2. Identify one benefit and one challenge when using each theory to guide your understanding of leadership or administrative practice within a social service organization.

Theory	Benefit	Challenge

3. What are the specific implications of these benefits and challenges for social work organizational leadership?

Implications

Leadership Exercise 3

Managing Differences

The following are elements of a philosophical stance regarding managing differences within an organizational setting. As a group, review each statement, discussing why you agree or disagree. Think about the implications for you as leaders in organizations peopled with professionals who are very different from you.

1. Both dominant and minority group members have been systematically exposed to misinformation about the majority and minority groups. This information will affect organizational behavior.

   Agree ___ Disagree___

   Why or why not?

   ____

   ____

2. Organizations work better for all concerned when stereotypes that devalue individuals' capacities and perspectives are eliminated.

   Agree ____ Disagree ____

   ____

   ____

3. In a multicultural environment, it is important to understand how powerful an influence culture is. One must recognize that one's own culture has its own set of interests, emotions, and biases before one can deal successfully with someone else's culture.

   Agree ____ Disagree ____

   ____

   ____

4. Taking advantage of the benefits of a multicultural environment means uncovering significant similarities and differences; recognizing contradictions, inconsistencies, and double standards; and avoiding oversimplifications.

   Agree ____ Disagree ____

   ____

   ____

Leadership Exercise 4

Organizational Assumptions

The following are assumptions about how organizations can or should work. As a group, review each statement, discussing why you agree or disagree. Then provide the implications for you as leaders in an organization peopled with professionals who are very different from you, holding different or opposing assumptions.

1. Organizations have a developmental cycle. Each stage in the cycle requires different skills and offers different opportunities to all those within the organization.

   Agree ____ Disagree ____

   ____

   ____

2. Organizations do not develop linearly and logically; instead, there is a good deal of circularity and serendipity.

   Agree ____ Disagree ____

   ____

   ____

3. Organizations are living organisms that can only be partially controlled. Instead of control, it is possible to find creativity, adaptability, and meaning within organizations.

   Agree ____ Disagree ____

   ____

   ____

4. Those working in an organization construct their vision of the organization. If they think it is oppressive, then it will be; if they think it is supportive, it will be. The same organization can be both oppressive and supportive to different employees at the same time. The meaning that employees find in organizations will shape their professional performance.

   Agree ____ Disagree ____

   ____

   ____

5. How one lives in an organization is a very personal undertaking. How one understands one's obligations and opportunities is also personal.

   Agree ____ Disagree ____

   ____

   ____

6. Collaboration, not just authority, is necessary for tasks and goal accomplishment within all segments of organizations.

   Agree ____ Disagree ____

   ____

   ____

7. Conflict, politics, power, authority, and leadership are all normal parts of organizational functioning.

   Agree ____ Disagree ____

   ____

   ____

8. For organizations to benefit fully from diversity it is necessary not only to recognize and deal with diversity, but also to celebrate it in order to capture its best potential. The question is how to do it.

   Agree ____ Disagree ____

   ____

   ____

9. There is no ideal structure or communication style within an organization, just as there is no mega theory or intervention to guide direct practice. What is necessary depends on the context and the circumstances at hand.

   Agree ____ Disagree ____

   ____

   ____

10. Organizations will progress with or without you. No one is indispensable within an organization.

    Agree ____ Disagree ____

    ____

    ____

Leadership Exercise 5

Ethical Leadership

Ethical leadership means weighing competing values and deciding how to approach a situation, knowing that a choice among values must be made. As a group, discuss how you would provide leadership in the following situations.

1. A supervisor for a private, not-for-profit, in-home health service that subsidizes services to isolated, poor, elderly individuals reviews a referral form from another agency, along with an application for subsidized in-home health services. The supervisor recognizes the name of the potential new client and realizes that the age stated on the forms is five years below the agency's eligibility standard for subsidized services. The supervisor approves the service request.

2. One foster-care supervisor for a public child welfare agency has interpreted policy to allow for providing vouchers to foster families to pay for additional costs related to extracurricular activities. Another foster-care supervisor has determined that the local budget cannot allow for such luxuries. Both supervisors know of the other's position, but have done nothing other than demand that their supervisees act according to their personal interpretation.

Ethical Leadership

Leadership Exercise 6

Mentoring New Workers

You are director of a small direct-service human service agency. Because your agency is small and you take every opportunity to serve the residents of the disadvantaged community in which the agency is located, most of your staff carry out multiple tasks.

You have a new staff member who is well-versed in behavioral intervention methods and is progressing very well in the agency. You have just assigned this new staff member an additional task of acting as liaison between a consumer-rights group and the agency. The group, which has titled itself "Por las Trabajadoras," seeks to change the discriminatory check cashing and consumer finance methods of local businesses. The staff member replies to your assignment very forthrightly, which you appreciate. The reply identifies a lack of experience in this type of community-oriented work and a certain fear of cultural and language barriers, although the worker does have enough knowledge to say, "No habla Español."

How would you help this worker develop the appropriate skills for this new assignment? Make certain that the worker can develop advocacy skills and begin to obtain cultural competence to facilitate working with this new consumer group. Share your thoughts with the class and see what others would do.

Leadership Exercise 7

Six-Month Evaluation: New Workers' Supervisory Conference

This exercise requires three small groups, each of which will have a role (described below). Each group will meet to plan the script for their role and to identify one person in the group to play the role. The group members who do not play the role become coaches, with specific duties during the actual role play. (Note: Only one member of your group will act in each role, but the other members may give advice during time-out periods that may be called by the principal role player.) Allow about 20 minutes of preparation time and 30 minutes for the role play itself.

The Situation

Family Service Agency (FSA) requires six-month evaluations of all clinical employees who have been with the agency for less than two years. After two years, workers move toward increased professional autonomy and have opportunities to participate in peer supervision, group supervision, and semiautonomous team functioning. However, during the first 24 months of professional employment the agency's policy emphasizes administrative accountability and professional growth through educational supervision. The agency has found that this policy has many benefits, including workers who earn various types of professional certification and professional recognition. The policy also tends to put workers into two categories—new, inexperienced clinicians (or "newclins") and experienced and autonomous workers ("topclins"). These categories, of course, carry status differences and result in certain organizational artifacts that at first may not be apparent to the causal observer. Staff turnover among the clinical staff results in newclins entering the agency fairly regularly. The turnover results not from dissatisfaction with the supervisory system or the agency position in the community. In fact, the agency is well regarded, and most professionals who have been employed at FSA recall their time there with fondness. Some of the turnover happens because the agency's professional staff is in high demand by better funded, larger agencies that recruit primarily the experienced workers who have been with the agency between four and eight years. Many of these workers leave when their families are growing and higher earnings opportunities become a critical matter for them.

One other piece of information will help you in planning the roles. The agency procedure calls for evaluation conference calls. The supervisor and the newclin are expected to independently develop three items for each conference. You will prepare each of these items for the role play.

1. First is an agenda—both the newclin and the supervisor separately create an agenda of the items they wish to cover during the conference, which is one hour long. The agendas are merged at the beginning of the conference, and agreement reached to delete or postpone some items if there seem to be too many items for the one-hour supervisory time period.
2. Second is an evaluation statement which emphasizes two things:
   - Evidence of progress in working toward semiautonomous practice.
   - Identification of issues that are barriers to progress.
3. Third is identifying accountability to the agency for competent practice. (Note that FSA prefers that measures of performance outcomes be employed, although it does not provide the criteria or standards.)

The Roles

Remember that only one member of your group will play the role, but the other members can give advice during time-out periods.

The Supervisor

You are a 55-year-old African-American female who holds an M.S.W. degree as well as an M.P.A. You are an experienced supervisor who has seen lots of newclins through the two-year new worker process, and most all of them have gone on to greater glory in the agency or elsewhere. To some degree, this stuff is old hat to you. You were probably the very model of a topclin before you became a supervisor, at least in your own mind, but you fumed once or twice recently when you overheard a reference to "old topclin"—you thought it was you about whom the reference was being made. At times like that, you ask yourself if you are losing touch with this up-and-coming generation.

The New Worker

You are a 28-year-old female of mixed Italian/African-American heritage. You are an inexperienced worker in this agency, although you had lots of experience after you obtained your B.S.W. degree and in your two challenging M.S.W. field placements. You worked for eight years in public social services, rising to direct an eligibility unit before returning to school for your M.S.W. degree. Your field placements in your master's program were in school social work and a juvenile correction facility as a substance-abuse counselor. This is your second supervisory conference in the agency. You thought after the first conference that you had been treated with little recognition of your experience, but you said nothing about this. Afterward, you listened to some of the newer topclins chatting over coffee about various supervisors, and you came to realize that your supervisor had a reputation for being a bit self-conscious about age and seemed to think that experience in the agency should bring status. You have also learned that your supervisor is regarded well in the agency for having led an organizational change effort that brought about increased services to the Hispanic community that was gradually moving into the agency's neighborhood.

Observer/Consultant

You are working for the consulting firm Experts, Inc. You have been hired to review the supervisory process at this agency, and you are authorized, among other things, to observe supervisory conferences at the agency. You have the ability to observe, listen in, and then interrupt the process when you think the process can be improved. However, your consulting style and your firm's guidelines do not allow you to give advice or direction; you may only ask leading questions intended to help the supervisor and supervisee to implement the supervisory conference constructively. In other words, you may stop the action and ask something like, "What did you expect to happen as a result of that question?" You may not say, "We think you should put that question in the form of a statement." Your team is made up of a diverse representation of experienced M.S.W.s.

Note that all of the observer/consultants participate, but only one of you may speak for the group. The non-speakers may give the speaker advice or coaching. Your assignment for the pre–role-play preparation is different from that of the other two roles. You will identify and list what principles and procedures for good supervisory conferences you want to look for in the supervisory conference you are going to observe. Also, identify how you will deliver your messages and comments to gain the greatest effectiveness. Your role is very important to the success of the exercise; your critical observation and constructive questioning will guide learning about supervisory evaluation. You also should establish a signal, and inform all participants of it, that will clearly indicate a "stop action" so that you may carry out your helping role with the supervisor and the newclin as they conduct the conference.

Debriefing

Following the role play, the entire group may want to discuss the following questions:

1. What are the differences between doing this role play and what you think might happen in the real world?
2. What did you observe about differences among the roles?
3. What did you observe about the similarities among the roles?
4. What principles of supervisory conferences emerged during the process?
5. What principles of professional work emerged in the process?
6. What other observations do you have?

Leadership Exercise 8

Interviewing Do's and Don'ts

Social work macro practice requires building and maintaining good relationships. The ability to carry out effective interviewing carries over into macro practice and effective macro practitioner behavior in relating to others often reflects effective interviewing skills. Below are basic "do and don't" lists for effective interviewing. In a group, discuss each, identifying how it can be applied in macro social work practice situations. How would you know when behaviors are at an acceptable standard of practice? Summarize your conclusions under each item.

The "DO" List

DO be cordial and receptive.

DO create a setting conducive to establishing a good relationship.

- Chairs that face each other convey a feeling of openness and equality.
- A desk can become a barrier to communication.

DO be aware of body language. Neatness of dress, posture, and facial expressions all send messages concerning what you really think and feel about the situation.

DO employ open-ended lead-in questions.

- This may mean allowing the interviewee to begin at his or her own starting point.
- Take your cues from that point.

DO be empathetic.

- Be natural.
- Be yourself.

DO move into interviewee's internal frame of reference so that they may tell you how they genuinely feel about the situation.

____

____

DO ask direct questions in order to obtain specific information.

____

____

DO use silence when appropriate. In effect you will be saying, "I am waiting and giving you time to develop your ideas clearly."

____

____

DO ask direct questions in order to obtain specific information.

____

____

DO repeat some of the interviewee's phrases exactly. This will allow you to explore more fully thoughts or feelings that the interviewee had begun to express.

____

____

DO be supportive. Reinforce the interviewee by letting the interviewee know that his or her thoughts, feelings, and opinions are important.

____

____

DO make the tasks to be accomplished a cooperative effort.

____

____

DO demonstrate that you believe in interviewees' capacities to use their own resources.

____

____

DO return to the central theme or presenting problem of the interview. This can be done by the use of an open-ended restatement: "You mentioned that Jimmy doesn't like his class . . ."

____

____

DO refer to other resources when appropriate.

____

____

DO be honest. Admit openly when you do not know an answer.

DO assume the appropriate share of the responsibility in carrying out agreed-upon goals.

DO summarize the highlights.

- Emphasize the explicit actions each of you will take in meeting the agreed-upon goals.
- Preferably, each party states their part in the action.
- This confirms, with clarity, the contract between them.

DO make a definite statement of the plans for follow-up and your next meeting.

DO be sincerely interested. Every word, gesture, and mannerism sends your message.

The "DON'T" List

DON'T be unfriendly or indifferent. Create a warm and friendly atmosphere.

DON'T ask a question beginning with "why." This puts the interviewee on the defense.

DON'T interrupt. Not only does this cut off the interviewee's thoughts; it is just plain rude.

DON'T intimidate or threaten. This confirms the lack of respect for the interviewee and is telling him or her that you see yourself as the only authority.

DON'T ridicule or be sarcastic. This enables the interviewee to be angry with you, and justifiably so.

DON'T use clichés. Clichés don't usually convey sincerity effectively.

DON'T show disbelief. If you do, you question the validity of the interviewee's statement.

DON'T use leading questions. Try to use indirect questions that avoid putting the interviewee on the defensive and avoid putting words in his or her mouth.

DON'T ask two questions at once. How is the interviewee to know which one to answer first?

DON'T convey the idea that the interviewee's ideas and techniques are unimportant by rejecting them.

DON'T use a double question, such as, "Now, is there something else?" or "Can we discuss the rest in the group meeting?" This places the interviewee in an either-or position, a bind that leaves no real alternative.

DON'T avoid the reality of the situation as the interviewee sees it. That is why he or she came to you in the first place.

DON'T scold.

DON'T allow other things (such as the telephone) to seem more important than the interview. If you do, you are telling the interviewee that you are not really interested in him or her.

DON'T tell the interviewee what to do. Instead, help the interviewee to arrive at a decision.

Leadership Exercise 9

Communication Inhibitors

Communication skills are critically important in any relationship. In group and team meetings, on task forces, in coalitions, and in supervisory relationships, some communication patterns can prevent your message from being heard. As a group, look at each of the areas below. Discuss examples of these communication barriers you have seen, and ways you might change these patterns. Write down notes and one real-life example or quote from your discussion, and share with the class how your group thinks these barriers can be avoided in order to enhance professional relationships.

Verbal Barriers to Effective Communication

Moralizing and sermonizing by using "shoulds" and "oughts."

- "You shouldn't have done that."
- "You're too young to get married."
- "You ought to pay your bills."

___

___

Passing judgment may cause others to be defensive, eliciting feelings of guilt and resentment. Advising or giving suggestions and solutions prematurely can be an inhibitor to good communication.

- "I suggest that you tell your colleague that you won't put up with him treating you that way."
- "I think that it would be best if you . . ."
- "Since your partner is always in trouble, why don't you look for new collaborators."

___

___

Persuading or giving logical arguments, lecturing, instructing, arguing, intellectualizing. These responses can provoke defensiveness and counterarguments. Don't ignore the feelings and views of the client.

- "Let's look at the facts about drugs."
- "Remember that you have some responsibility for solving problems too."
- "That attitude won't get you anywhere."

___

___

Judging, criticizing, or placing blame. In making negative judgments, you violate the basic social work values of nonjudgmental attitudes and acceptance.

- "You are wrong about that."
- "Not attending that meeting was a bad mistake."

Analyzing, diagnosing, making glib or dramatic interpretations, labeling others' behaviors. These responses put you in a one-up position and defines others as in need of corrective input. They also label people.

- "You're behaving that way because you are mad at the world."
- "Your attitude is causing you a lot of problems."

Reassuring, sympathizing, consoling, excusing. Well-timed reassurance can encourage hope, but responding only at the surface level prevents others from self-knowledge and exploration. You may be reassuring only yourself.

- "You'll feel better tomorrow."
- "I really feel sorry for you."
- "Don't worry, things will work out."

Using sarcasm or employing humor that is distractive or makes light of others' problems. Humor can be a useful tool, but not if it keeps the content at a superficial level. Sarcasm often comes from hostility and the client will sense this.

- "Get up on the wrong side of the bed?"
- "You really are a sucker for falling for that line."

Threatening, warning, or counterattacking. These responses often promote unwillingness of people to look at their own behavior.

- "If you don't . . . you will be sorry."
- "You better . . . or else."

Leadership Exercise 10

Asking Questions

Ineffective questions usually fall into one of three categories:

1. Closed-ended questions, such as "Are you getting along ok?" By contrast, "Can you tell me what you have been experiencing since you arrived yesterday?" allows an expanded and richer response as the person is free to respond from a much broader domain.
2. Stacking questions. These blur focus and are confusing! "How is your relationship with Jane? Is that one of your biggest priorities, or is there another that concerns you?"
3. Leading questions, that is, questions with a hidden agenda. Examples are: "Do you think you have really tried to get along with your colleague?" "Aren't you too young to move into that position?" These may induce people to agree with your view or adopt your belief.

As a group, think about how questions can be used to either facilitate or inhibit communication. Design two brief role plays for each of the following types of questioning, illustrating how one might ask a question inappropriately and then how each might be reframed.

1. Interrupting inappropriately or excessively. This can annoy people, stifle spontaneous expressions, and hinder exploration.
2. Dominating interaction. No need to assume all initiative for discussion.
3. Fostering social interaction. Growth-producing relationships are characterized by sharp focus and specificity (concreteness). This, however, does not mean you shouldn't make a person comfortable.
4. Responding passively. You may need to provide form and direction to maximize the helping process.
5. Parroting or overusing certain phrases or clichés. Remember that it is important to respond creatively.
6. Dwelling on the remote past. Focusing largely on the present is vital because people can change only their present circumstances, behavior, and feelings.
7. Using self-disclosure prematurely. Self-disclosure is appropriate only when you are clear about how many people may benefit from your response. Does it make you more real as a person or does it serve your own personal needs?

Leadership Exercise 11

Team Analysis

Participating in and leading teams is a major activity for macro social work practitioners. Understanding and enhancing team skills can make you more effective in leadership roles. Naomi Brill (1976)[1] identified key questions to help us understand teams; this approach has been adapted below.

Have a group of five to seven people volunteer to be in a "fishbowl" role play. Select a topic or develop a role-play situation in which they will participate. Topics might include a current issue in the local, national, or international news (and its resolution), an organizational dilemma faced by one of the team members, or even a concern the students have about their university or college. The remainder of the class can use the following questions to observe team dynamics. Have at least two to three people focus on each of the following categories: (1) purpose, (2) composition and structure, (3) internal social system, (4) administration and logistics, (5) internal process, and (6) environment.

Purpose

1. What is the function of this team?

____

____

2. Who defined it?

____

____

3. Is there common understanding and agreement regarding its meaning?

____

____

4. Can its function be changed? By whom?

____

____

5. Have working goals grown out of it?

____

____

[1]Brill, N. (1976). *Teamwork: Working together in the human services.* Philadelphia: Lippincott.

Composition and Structure

6. Who makes up the team?

____

____

7. How is this decided?

____

____

8. How were/are members selected?

____

____

9. How is membership changed?

____

____

10. What is done to enable individuals to become participating team members?

____

____

11. How are the roles of the team members initially defined?

____

____

12. How are roles changed in process?

____

____

13. Is there clear and common understanding of team composition and structure among the members?

____

____

Internal Social System

14. What is the underlying value system of the team?

____

____

15. What are the behavioral norms of this team?

____

____

16. How do they relate to institutional, community, and societal values and norms?

17. How are the norms enforced, evaluated, and changed?

18. What is the culture of this team?

19. How is it maintained and changed?

20. Where does the power in this team lie?

21. How is power manifested and used?

22. How is power controlled and changed?

23. What are the pressures that may lead to groupthink in this team?

24. How are pressures managed?

Administration and Logistics

25. How is the team managed?

26. How does leadership take place?

27. How are leadership and administration related?

28. From where do resources for the team's function come? How?

29. What are the essential logistics of this team's operation?

30. Who provides support and maintenance services?

31. What provisions exist for ongoing evaluation and change?

Internal Process

32. How do team members communicate among themselves?

33. Is there a common language, including professional terms?

34. Is there provision for recognizing and working to clear communication problems?

35. How does the team initiate discussions?

36. How does the team use conflict?

37. How does this team reach decisions?

38. How do the members of this team collaborate, accept, and implement decisions, both those they support and those with which they disagree?

39. How does the team use authority?

40. How are individual and team tasks defined and implemented?

41. Does the team consciously use a problem-solving process?

42. If so, how does it deal with breakdowns in this process?

43. What is the arrangement for necessary supervision of the team and its members?

44. How does the team evaluate itself and its members?

45. How is the effectiveness of team members and their accomplishments assessed?

Environment

46. What constitutes the team's external environment?

47. What relationships are involved?

48. What are the channels of communication to the external environment?

49. What happens along the interfaces of the various elements in the environment?

50. What are the linkages with these various elements?

51. How are these linkages used?

52. How are they evaluated and changed?

53. How is this team accountable to those who sanction its work: clients, institution, community, society?

Finally, ask yourself if you would want to be a member of this team. Why or why not?

Leadership Exercise 12

Long-Term-Care Advocates

Originally conceived in the early 1970s, The Long Term Care Ombudsman Program (LTCOP) emerged from demonstration projects in five states. In 1975, grants were provided to most states for ombudsman program development, and by 1978, each state was required to establish and operate a statewide ombudsman program. The program's original purpose was to respond to complaints from residents, families, staff, and others involved in nursing-home facilities in the United States. Subsequently, the purpose expanded to include the monitoring of board and care, assisted living, and even home-care programs in some states.

The federally mandated LTCOP is an example of how a public mandate is implemented through the use of paid and volunteer ombudsmen performing under both public and private auspices. There are several hundred paid ombudsmen at the state and local levels, as well as thousands of volunteers who are recruited and trained to represent the ombudsman program. Volunteers comprise 90% of ombudsmen. Over the last decade, a number of studies have focused on various aspects of the Long Term Care Ombudsman Program. In addition, a number of monographs, reports, and conceptual analyses have focused on the need for increased program accountability. One study by the Institute on Medicine recommended that mechanisms be developed to better document the efforts of ombudsmen.

The program's mandate, through the Older Americans Act, requires ombudsmen to investigate complaints in long-term-care facilities, but data have not been systematically collected to document what paid and volunteer ombudsmen do in their daily work. The Administration on Aging must only report aggregate numbers of complaints to decision makers at the national level. There is no national database that can be used for analyzing what really happens in long-term-care settings around the country, who investigated the complaints, who complained, and how complaints were resolved. Because the complaint-reporting system is pivotal to what ombudsmen do, it has been viewed with concern over the past few years. Each state is required by law to develop a systematic reporting system, but this requirement has not been closely monitored. Some states have computerized systems and others have very limited reporting methods.

Given the nature of this program, think about how client advocacy, cause advocacy, legislative advocacy, and administrative advocacy are relevant to the LTCOP. Here are some questions to begin a group discussion about this program.

- How might client advocacy be relevant? Would individual volunteer ombudsmen be engaged in client advocacy? What would that look like? What examples could you identify?
- How might cause advocacy be relevant? When might client advocacy become cause advocacy? What kinds of issues might require cause advocacy? What examples can you provide?
- How might legislative advocacy be relevant? When might cause advocacy require legislative advocacy and what would this look like? What examples can you provide?
- How about administrative advocacy? Think about advocacy from both the LTCOP's perspective, as well as if you were in a long-term-care facility. How would internal and external change differ in these situations?
- Given the questions you have addressed above, how might strategies and tactics vary?
- What is your preferred strategy and why?

Leadership Activities

Leadership Activity A

Providing Leadership

Social workers have leadership responsibilities within any organization in which they work; leadership is not just vested in a title or position. Leadership is an attitude about responsibilities in an organization based on a set of social work values and skills that compel a person to act.

The following is an analytic activity to help you identify what it takes to feel able to act when change is necessary. Respond in as much detail as possible to the questions and use either your field placement site or your employing agency as the organizational context for this work.

1. Given my personality, world view, and work experience, what do I need to feel both comfortable and competent in my organization?

2. Given the mission, history, size, employee base, and client needs, what does the organization need from me? What kind of leadership (formal, informal, assigned, conferred) is acceptable when taking action as an internal change agent?

3. Given what I know about myself and the organization, how can I provide leadership in:

   - Assuring that my job contributes to the goals of the organization?

   - Assuring that client outcomes are achieved?

- Assuring that my colleagues are also working toward client and organizational goals?

____

____

- Assuring that high ethical standards are achieved and maintained in the organization?

____

____

Leadership Activity B

Macro-Practice Roles

Sometimes future macro practitioners wonder about the type of positions for which they will be qualified when they enter the employment market. Look in the employment section of your local newspaper and select employment ads that might be potential opportunities for macro social work graduates to pursue.

See if you can find ads for each of the following roles, in various types of organizations:

- Administrator
- Advocate
- Budget analyst
- Consultant
- Coordinator
- Development officer/specialist
- Director
- Finance director
- Fund-raiser
- Human resource specialist
- Leader
- Manager
- Marketer
- Planner
- Program developer
- Program specialist
- Policy analyst
- Social program planner
- Teacher
- Trainer
- Supervisor

Are there other roles for which you have skills? If so, list those roles here and find ads to match.

____

____

____

____

Assess the ads. Are they looking specifically for a social worker, or will your skills or values match the ad regardless of the discipline requested? What are your conclusions?

____

____

Are the employment settings traditional human-service organizations? How do you know?

____

____

What other types of settings did you find?

Would a nontraditional setting, such as the power company or an animal shelter, be an acceptable venue for exercising social work leadership?

Leadership Activity C

Preferred Tactics

Leaders need to choose approaches that sometimes require them to go outside their comfort zone. Provide definitions for the following approaches to change:

- Collaborative tactics

____

____

- Campaign tactics

____

____

- Contest tactics

____

____

Now discuss the costs and benefits of each approach.

____

____

____

____

____

What type of change situations would be most amenable to each?

____

____

____

____

____

____

In order for you to engage in each of these tactics with equal competence, what knowledge, skills, or attitudes will you need to acquire or change?

Leadership Activity D

Persuasive Leadership

Imagine that you have become aware of a proposal aimed at creating a major change in the child day-care licensing law. Essentially, the proposal is to eliminate all restrictions and standards for those providing care for children other than their own, whether they are providing home- or center-based care. The standards that will remain are those zoning, and health and safety standards that would apply when nonrelated persons occupy the same building. No expectations regarding adult/child ratios, educational, developmental, or nutritional standards will be specified. This proposed change comes out of a belief that by eliminating the barriers to providing care, more day-care slots will become available in the state. Further, it is believed that acceptable standards beyond health and safety will be maintained because the consumers of the day-care service will make appropriate demands for quality care and select providers who provide quality care.

You see yourself as a child advocate even though that is not part of your current job description. However, because of your strong position regarding this proposal, you feel the need to make your voice heard. You choose to make your voice heard in the public discourse concerning the policy.

Record what happens when you take the following steps in order to exert your professional and personal leadership:

1. Select your favorite model of policy analysis and apply it to the proposed policy. Write a statement identifying your position regarding the policy, being sure that you can defend your opinion.

___

___

2. If full analysis is not possible because of gaps in the information, identify the essential questions that would need answers. Think about what your position might be, given the range of possible answers.

___

___

3. What might be a reasonable strategy to get your position into the public discourse? What would the costs and benefits be of:

   - Letter writing?
   - Connecting with legislators?
   - Organizing?
   - Marching?
   - Other options?

4. What would be your preferred strategy?

___

___

5. Given your position, what might be the future course of this policy if it was adopted?

6. What additional skills would you need to use (or develop) to be certain that the policy shaping and implementation took your desired direction?

Leadership Activity E

Interviewing Outline

You will participate in an interview process many times in macro practice. Below is a guide that will facilitate the interviewing process. Use this guide to interview someone in your field agency, place of employment, or in an organization with which you are familiar.

Determine the purpose of the interview. Be sure that the interviewee understands the purpose.

Begin Interview
- Begin where the person is.
- Attempt to set the interviewee at ease.
- Observe the comfort of the interviewee.
- Make efforts to establish rapport.

Show Interest
- Show courtesy throughout the interview.
- Treat the person with dignity.
- Individualize the process.

Project Warmth
- Attend to tone in voice.
- Demonstrate sincerity of involvement.
- Show attentiveness and make eye contact (if culturally appropriate).
- Remain person-centered, not note-centered.

Draw Out Affect
- Encourage the interviewee to express feelings such as anger, sadness, warmth, joy, despair, hostility, and so on.
- Use skill in responding to attitudes and behaviors.

Recognize Cues
- Recognize and use appropriate verbal communication.
- Recognize and use appropriate nonverbal communication.

Maintain Consistent Role
- Clarify roles.
- Be consistent in your role.

Use Self-Control
- Recognize your own stress, prejudice, and judgmental feelings.
- Convey your purpose in the interview.

Use Questioning Techniques
- Maintain proper balance between general and specific questions.
- Use probes that facilitate the other person telling their story in their own words.

Use Good Listening Techniques
- Recognize the proper use of silence to encourage the other person to talk.
- Respond nonverbally as appropriate.

Ending the Interview

- Briefly summarize interview content.
- Provide opportunity for feedback on interview process.
- Explain any future plan/view in regard to follow-up.

After the interview, evaluate how it went. What would you have done differently? What would you have done the same? What do you want to work on for future interviewing?

Leadership Activity F

Emergency Preparedness: Assessing Your Organization for Community Response

It is important for social service agencies to build and maintain the capacity for responding to community emergency situations. Emergency contingency operation plans can contribute to an organization's ability to respond and function during community-wide emergencies. This activity provides an opportunity to assess organizational capacity for continuing to operate during emergencies and for meeting community needs in crisis situations.

Below is an outline of key factors to take into account in measuring the preparedness status of human-service organizations. From your field-instruction agency or the social service organization in which you work, obtain its emergency-preparedness plan. Then apply these key factors to determine how prepared the organization is for continuing operations under emergency conditions.

Determining if an emergency exists: Response priorities

- Are response priority levels defined?
- Is there a code system to communicate the severity of the situation and the corresponding response?
- Who determines severity and declares the level of emergency?

Activating an emergency response: Contingency operations plan

- Is there a written plan?
- Who has possession of the plan?
- What does it say regarding communication with and between employees?
- What does it say about decision-making responsibilities?
- What does it say about service delivery?
- What does it say about documentation of services?
- What does it say about protection of records?
- What does it say about protection of staff?
- What does it say about protection of clients?
- What does it say about service delivery at alternative sites?
- What does it say about protection/utilization of necessary equipment?
- What does it say about notification of the public?
- What does it say about testing the plan through "dry runs"?

Continuing service during times of emergency: Continuing action

- Are the roles and responsibilities of administration and staff clearly stated?
- What about backup and relief? Daily briefings?
- Is there an emergency organization chart?
- Is there a plan for accepting/managing/distributing donations?
- Are there arrangements for staff maintenance if required to work extended hours? What about their families?
- Is there a review schedule in order to adjust the plan when necessary?

Action during extreme emergency

- Are there instructions regarding how to proceed if a staff person or client is missing?
- Is it clear what to do if there is catastrophic destruction?
- Is it clear what to do if there is loss of life?
- Do plans include mechanisms to help staff deal with the stress involved in dealing with disasters?

If a plan does not exist, how would you assure that one is developed and adopted within your agency?

Leadership Activity G

Job Search

Take a few moments to describe the position that would be ideal for you as your first post-graduation job. Articulate the duties, responsibilities, field of practice, agency type, challenges, and special rewards that you want at this point in your professional development.

If you do not obtain this ideal position, what would be an acceptable alternative? List elements in the position you consider critical.

Are there any types of positions or settings that would be intolerable or unacceptable for your first position after graduation? Once you have written this, analyze for themes that emerge for you to explore further.

What salary and benefit package do you have in mind for your first position?

Do you have geographical limitations on where you seek employment?

What are the trade-offs necessary for you to change any of your salary, benefit, or location requirements?

What strategies will you use to help you keep up with developments in social work and in your special areas of practice?

What additional skill packages do you think you will need in order for you to meet client, staff, and colleague needs in the most effective way possible?

What is the second position you would like to have? Describe it here.

How long do you see yourself waiting until you seek this second position?

___

___

___

___

"The Days of Our Placement: Postscript

Tamara returned to her rural community, worked for two years as a child welfare program worker and liaison to the State Child Welfare Services Planning Committee. She currently heads up a special rural child welfare project for the Child Welfare League of America, working out of Atlanta.

Chrystal decided to see the world and spent two years in the Peace Corps in Costa Rica. She reported to the others that all those years of high school and college Spanish really enhanced her social work career when she went on to work in Latin America for the Christian Children's Fund. When last heard from, she was setting up a pilot children's aid program in Yemen.

Yusof settled in a suburb of Washington, DC after meeting another recent social work M.S.W. graduate who was employed by a mosque there. Yusof helped establish the mosque's new social service program. He worked for subsistence wages only for 18 months, before starting his own consulting firm. He is now executive director of a national association whose mission is to strengthen community services for American Muslims.

Maria and Harry had actually been off working together—and more—during those last weeks at the agency. They returned to New York after working as community organizers with Native Americans in the West. Harry is lobbying the city, elected officials, and the National Park Service to create a restored settlement house on the Upper East Side. Maria is service director for the city's largest community after-school child-care program. Thanks to her efforts, the program has a sliding-fee scale and grant funding for scholarships. Maria and Harry's twin boy and girl are regular attendees at the program.